Eolithic Homiletics
by
Charles R. Wilson

Published by BioWrite
A company owned by Charlene Rose Johnson
14971 SE 107th Ave, Summerfield, FL 34491

It is the policy of BioWrite to print the books we publish on acid-free paper and in the best environmental methods we know.

Wilson, Charles R.
        Eolithic Homiletics: Charles R. Wilson

ISBN: 978-0-615-63059-5

Printed in the United States of America

First Edition

Book Design by Kace Montgomery

Published by BioWrite   a subsidiary of Charlene Rose Johnson

The Church is a community in ministry
not
A community gathered around a minister!

Wesley Frensdorff

It's the people telling their stories
that
Gives the Gospel its wings to fly

Bishop Kivengere

DEDICATION

This Volume is dedicated to the Glory of God
and in Thanksgiving for the Joy and Company of Children.

And to:

Charlene Rose, William (Bill) Keith, Deborah Gail and Sharon Lynn

who have enriched my life immeasurably and provided
many blessings on my journey and ministry.

And in the Same Spirit:
A Huge Thanks to my Family for Encouragement in this Project
Especially:
> *Bill, computer technician; Charlene, Author; and*
> *Lee Moore, Journalist (and former spouse)*

…whose generous and gracious aid were essential.

TABLE OF CONTENTS

Contents listed are shown as:
Part One: MAJOR ESSAYS
Part Two: SERMONS
     Short Themes
(See Foreword for More Detail)

FOREWORD

The purpose of this volume is to provide congregations with
a resource and justification for the development of a ministry of
preaching in which preaching is known as a proper function of
baptismal ministry rather than the exclusive prerogative of the
ordained. In advocating greater recognition of baptismal ministry I
stand in the line of such prophets as Roland Allen, Carlyle Marney,
Wesley Frensdorff and many others who have championed this cause.

A major portion of the material presented herein derives from
my twelve year, part-time role as rector of Intercession Episcopal
Church in Thornton, Colorado. During that time a church initially
threatened with closure as "nonviable" built and moved into a brand
new facility; became and continues to be a vital, witnessing presence
in its community and diocese. More importantly, the theory and
practice of ministry advocated herein was and is demonstrated by the
saints of Intercession. I am grateful for having been a part of their
story.

Part One of this book consists of four Chapters on Parochial
Leadership. The first chapter, Eolithic Homiletics considers the roots
of the title; what, exactly is meant by "Eolithic?" Since the question
of authority will loom large in the minds of some who may review
the case presented herein, the second chapter, Authority; Theory
and Practice, presents an argument for the intrinsic duty of laity to
witness formally to their faith. A more embracing issue is leadership
in general. This is addressed in the third chapter Properties of
Leadership. Finally there may be the question of how one actually gets
started with a broad based ministry of preaching. A few suggestions
will be found in the fourth chapter, Developing the Parochial Base.

The main body of material (Part Two) is a selection of Sermons
which I hope will serve as sample material to help anyone mystified
by what I've attempted to say in Part One. Finally, I'm including
several short items such as you might find in someone's column in
a parish newsletter. These will, I hope, further illustrate the case for
Eolithic Leadership.

Alone?

The author was trying to express the probable attitude of the disciples after the crucifixion. Gathered together, frightened, in a closed room they might have said, "Is he going to leave us alone?" meaning, "Does he expect us to handle everything on our own—with no help?" But for one fleeting instant I read it, "Is he finally going to leave us alone, off the hook—quit bugging us?"

For just an instant, then I saw the intended meaning. But it was enough to set both questions up in my mind and to see the answer to both: "No." Of course he would not leave us "on our own." That was the author's rhetorical question to set the disciples up for Pentecost. But the second question . . .

I have this framed copy of a photo. I've kept it in my study for years. Perhaps you've seen it; a pattern of black and white splotches like someone's idea of an inkblot test. The story that goes with the photo is this. Many years ago a Chinese student with much trouble in his heart concerning religion, took a picture of melting snow on a mountain. As he developed the print in the tray, all that came out was the white snow and the contrasting black areas where the mountain was bare. But in this pattern of black and white he suddenly saw quite clearly the head of Christ and was converted to Christianity.

I've observed many people responding to this photo. At first glance they see splotches; "abstract art" they think. Then I explain and they look again. Sometimes it takes a few minutes—straining doesn't help—but when they relax and let it happen, sort of like faith, they see the face. It may take months, then one day, unexpectedly, the face startles them. I suppose, for some it never happens. But there is one point that does seem to hold: Once you see him, you can never, not see him again.

Is he going to leave us alone? Sometimes when we're feeling the overwhelming burden of our responsibilities; when we've had all we can bear, the question comes "Are we on our own?" and the answer is "No." The power will be given to see it through. And sometimes when the cause seems lost, the road impenetrable and the questions come, "Can we get out of it? Will he quit bugging us?"

Again the answer is an emphatic "No!" For once you've seen him you can never-ever not see him again.

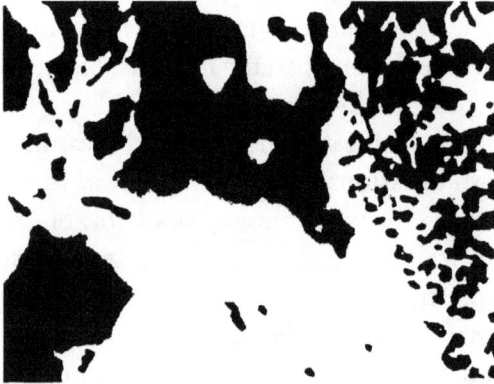

No word is the Word of God
Unless…
It is the Word of God for Someone
— Paul Tillich

PART ONE

EOLITHIC HOMILETICS

AUTHORITY:
THEORY & PRACTICE

PROPERTIES OF LEADERSHIP

DEVELOPING THE PARISH BASE

EOLITHIC HOMILETICS

Planning is big on the world's agenda these days. We hear of Urban Planning, Business Planning, Five Year Plans. It was in this environment that I was initially called into the church's planning agenda. I learned that planning is a rational, lineal, one step at a time, process. My challenge was to figure out what Church planning should be. I had this wild notion that since God is Creator, God had to have been the Original Planner. The question then became: "What kind of planner is God?" Surely Church Planning should be based on the same principles as the Eternal Planning Process. So began my quest: to understand the nature of God's planning process. As my search began I stumbled onto a label that caught the essence of what I sought: Eolithic Planning!

A few years ago, about the time when Christmas catalogues began to appear, I was browsing through one of them that had a lot of artsy–craftsy stuff in it. I wasn't looking for anything to purchase, rather for some project ideas for my wood working hobby. I spotted one that grabbed me. It was a walnut plaque with a decorative, routed border and a simple carving of a cat on the surface. It was a replica of an old hobo sign from the depression era, when those knights of the road roamed the neighborhood looking for a meal or rode the rails to the next town looking for work. They had a sign language designed to help each other along the way. Symbols could be scratched on a board fence or sidewalk. One of them was a simple sketch of a kitty, and the message it bore was, "home of a kind-hearted woman."

I came up with some scraps of walnut in my shop, edge-glued three of them, cut the piece to size, routed the decorative edge and carved the hobo cat on the face of the plaque. I had no idea what I was going to do with the thing. However, as I was hand rubbing it to a fine, oiled finish, an idea struck me. At the time we had a woman in a nursing home dying of cancer. Clair had been a woodworker. For many months she had lived in Olive's spare room. Both women were widows, had been close friends for years, and Olive had become the devoted caregiver for Clair. As Clair's cancer advanced, it became necessary to move her into a nursing home. Of course Olive visited her at least daily and I was keeping pretty close track of things. Anyway, as I was rubbing that plaque, its purpose hit me in a flash. I would take it to Clair, neatly boxed, ready for gift wrapping and say, "Clair, as one wood worker to another, it occurred to me that you might like to have something special for Olive for Christmas." I enclosed a little card that explained the hobo message. Clair died before Christmas.

Sometime after Christmas I saw Olive and, with a tear in her eye, she showed me the hobo plaque. In Eolithic Planning the purpose doesn't have to go in first; it's just as natural for it to come along later.

If you were to visit the Anglican Cathedral in Victoria, British Columbia, stood somewhere near the crossing, then stretched your neck to peer up into that vaulted ceiling, you just might spot a stone carving of a robin sitting on a nest. I suppose many a worshipper over the years has discovered that insignificant, little example of a stone carver's artistic talent perched way up there atop a main column, and wondered. The story is this: When the cathedral was under construction, after the columns were in place but way before the building was closed in, a pair of robins built a nest on top of one of the main columns and proceeded to raise their brood.

EOLITHIC HOMILETICS

The stone masons simply moved their work to the other end of the site for the next few weeks so as not to disturb the birds. Once the young robins had fledged, the masons continued with their work at the crossing and of course the nest had to be removed. However one of the masons made a stone carving of a robin sitting on a nest and fixed it in place on top of that column. In Eolithic Planning it's perfectly natural for a robin to help in the design a cathedral.

Mark's literary style is that he regularly has Jesus setting off to do something, then being interrupted by something else. A man with an unclean spirit interrupts his teaching in the synagogue; a paralyzed man is lowered through the roof interrupting his teaching in the house. His rest is interrupted to feed the five thousand; his prayer time is interrupted to save his followers on a raging sea. He is interrupted while traveling, while eating, while teaching and at prayer. According to Mark, one could almost say that Jesus' ministry of teaching, healing, feeding and saving was more a function of the interruptions than of the plans. Ministry too is Eolithic!

One of the key characteristics of Eolithic Planning is its playfulness. Play is associated with a striving for excellence, for its creativity and its willingness to risk looking foolish. It's nearly the opposite of "work." Work is usually associated with drudgery, monotony and face-saving maneuvers. Some examples:

Years ago I took a job with our national church center in New York City. This necessitated a move from Idaho to (in order to preserve some of our western life style), an acreage in rural New Jersey. With that, we could keep our horses and I would simply have to commute by rail to the city. Our small town railroad station was within walking distance of our home. The railroad was the Jersey Central. Now in those days the Jersey Central was tired, worn out and poorly maintained. Things were so bad that one morning on our way to the city we actually ran out of fuel and the local oil dealer was called in to "fill 'er up." Whether you were an employee or a passenger, this railroad was drudgery, boredom and dullsville; a total "work" situation.

In sharp contrast to most of the stations up and down the line which were boarded up, crumbling and rotting away, our little station was in a fine state of repair, freshly painted, flower beds well maintained; inside, beautiful framed photos of the romantic days of railroading hung on the walls. The whole thing looked as it must have in the early nineteen hundreds; the difference? Our station had been leased to the High Iron Company, a railroad buff's club. The Club owned an ancient steam locomotive and an assortment of passenger cars, all of them parked on the side and everything maintained far beyond anything owned by the Jersey Central.

Every once in a while club members would gather on a Saturday and go for a ride. "Railroaders" would dress in their bib overalls and railroader's caps, "grease" smeared on their faces and big red handkerchiefs hanging out of their back pockets. As they pulled into the station the "conductor" would swing down, wipe the hand rail with his handkerchief and place the wooden step stool on the ground for the convenience of the "passengers." As the train pulled into the station from the east (a slight upgrade) other club members would be found on the side of the track, tape recording the throaty "chugs" of that old steam engine.

So, this is the story of two railroads. One is work. One is play! I can remember when I was a kid; railroading was in its glorious youth. There was pride and joy in railroading in those days, and a striving for excellence. The spirit of play was in it. But that spirit has escaped. Railroading is now drudgery. We can see the same thing happening with the airlines today. What do we have to do to keep the spirit of play in our transportation, our industry, our government, in our church?

I said that creativity is associated with play. Inventors have to be a playful lot. Picture Thomas Edison in his New Jersey lab. See the Wright brothers in their bicycle shop. Don't you get a picture of men at play? When the Spaniards first got to Central America they discovered that the Indians had invented a form of the wheel. However they used it for their children's toys. It had never occurred to them to build a cart and make hauling their fire wood easier. The Chinese invented gun powder and the compass. They used the gun powder for fireworks and the compass to determine the proper orientation for a grave. These were activities we would associate with play. It never occurred to them to build cannon, or to use the compass for navigation.

Finally, I associated play with the willingness to risk looking foolish. One of the refrains in the Gospel is "Blessed is he who takes no offense at me." In other words, the opposite of faith is not unbelief. The opposite of faith is offense – looking foolish. When one confronts the Christ, one responds in faith, or in offense. (No response shows that the confrontation was missed altogether.) People of faith don't mind the risk of looking foolish; that's the playful part of it.

I once went to a large regional church meeting where part of the agenda was to come up with a plan to feed the hungry of the world's impoverished nations. An enormous challenge! Well, the discussion went on and what was beginning to emerge was a plan that called for church members to fast one day each week. The savings in cash that that would represent would then be contributed to Church World Services or some group engaged in feeding the hungry. The compelling aspect of the plan was that in our day of fasting we would be sharing in a small way in the hunger of the world. Of course the other side of that fast would be an actual contribution to the feeding of the hungry. I watched in particular a seminary student who had joined us, and who appeared to be embarrassed by all this. We couldn't hope to make a dent in the hunger of the world and this was obvious. He had a better idea; triage.

So he explained to an attentive audience how triage worked on the battlefield in caring for the wounded. His application to feeding the world's hungry would work like this: determine which third of the nations would probably make it without help and skip them. Figure out which third would not likely make it even with substantial help and scratch them. Finally, consider which third might possibly benefit from our help, and concentrate our efforts there. He looked around at his fellow church members, confident that he had come up with the best plan. They turned back to their discussion, without comment, of the one day a week fast. They were not offended; they would simply take their basketful of loaves and fishes and go feed the five thousand anyway. That's Eolithic Planning; a blissful willingness to risk looking foolish; joyful creativity and energetic striving for excellence. It's right for the church.

I suggested earlier that I'd been studying, playing with, teaching and writing about some of these ideas for a long time. Many years ago while on this quest, I ran into a book that helped me tie it all together. Purposive Systems was a collection of essays that came out of a meeting of Cyberneticists. The essay that caught my attention was The Nature of Purpose by then Boulder, Colorado professor of philosophy, David Hawkins. According to Hawkins there are two kinds of purposive activity. One we readily recognize, the other we seldom notice.

The first he calls "design." Suppose our plan shows a highway crossing a certain ravine. Our design challenge in this case is to get the highway across that ravine so it can continue on the other side. So we study the site, take measurements and design the bridge on paper. Later, engineers study our plan, order up the materials, and erect the bridge in accordance with the specs. In this process, the purpose goes in up front. The material and work follow in an orderly sequence; needs come first and push the process, the effect is experienced later.

The second process Hawkins calls "Eolithic." An eolith is something that is discovered or stumbled upon, not something created for a purpose. The purpose is seen in retrospect. It might be a remnant or a scrap of something left over from some other project; probably cast aside by some designer. A potsherd found in an old dig might turn out to make an excellent scrapper. Imagine an early caveman wandering somewhere in a field with nothing in particular on his mind. At some point he spots a peculiar looking stone about the size of his fist. Curiosity compels him to examine it. He turns it over and studies it from various angles. One might even say he admires it insofar as this might be considered a function of his dim mind. Then an idea strikes him. He finds a stick of about the

EOLITHIC HOMILETICS

right size and, with some rawhide fixes the stone to one end of the stick. He has invented the lever and created a stone ax. Now he can crack skulls, human or other, and has a technological advantage over everybody else, for a little while. Now notice this; in this process there was no up-front purpose – the purpose came into the picture later; like me carving a hobo sign.

But notice this also; the "cause" might have been teleological. That is, instead of the cause being a force from behind that pushes things, it might have been a signal out front calling forth. Teleological thinking is not allowed in science. And I certainly agree with that – in science. But teleological thinking is surely a proper part of theological reasoning. For example, we could not say (scientifically speaking) "the rains came because the prairie was in a drought and the wells were drying up." That wouldn't be allowed. Scientifically, we have to explain the rains in terms of some preceding cause; a weather front moved in or something. However theologically speaking we could claim that "the rains came because the little church out on the prairie had been praying for rain for weeks." That's teleological thinking that's theologically justified. The little church was out front calling forth, not behind, pushing. Let's note in passing that with Eolithic thinking prayer is a natural and even rational part of routine procedures, not some strange superstitious practice left over from bygone days.

Something like this happens when a bird builds a nest or a beaver constructs a dam. Those creatures don't sit down and draw up a plan in advance. As they build they have no sense of purpose up front. We say they do it by instinct, but we could also explain it as an Eolithic process. I do believe that somewhere deep inside people there are receptors capable of picking up signals that we are hardly aware of, and we respond, not really knowing what we are doing or why we are doing it. So thanks to David Hawkins, I now had a name for a process I was beginning to understand. I would call it Eolithic Planning.

So that brings us to an obvious question: what is the ultimate nature of creativity? What kind of a planner-creator is God? As we prepare to ponder the nature of God as creator, our western cultural proclivities lead us automatically to assumptions of God as Eternal Designer. After all, we can examine the structure of space and time; it looks like the work of a designer. But there is more. I see a Playful Creator, an Eolithic Creator. And I get this, at least partly, from scripture. Consider the six days of creation for starters. Each day God takes on a different project and says "Let it be." Then, we are told, "It was so." Then God backs off to admire his work and observes, "Wow that's pretty darn good!" You see, he surprised himself. He apparently didn't know in advance how it would turn out. That's an Eolithic Process.

Or consider this from the book of Job (Chapter 38) God is scolding Job:

Where were you when I laid the foundation of the earth?
Tell me if you have understanding
Who determined its measurements – surely you know
Or who stretched the line upon it?
On what were its bases sunk, or who laid its corner stone?

So far it sounds like a designer, doesn't it? But listen;

When the morning stars sang together
And all the sons of God shouted for joy?

Surely it's an Eolithic process.

Or, this from Psalm 104:

Oh look—the deep, wide sea, brimming with fish past counting.
Ships plow those waters, and Leviathan, your pet dragon
romps in them.

There are many others, but I am convinced that ultimate creativity is rooted in play and that God is the Original Eolithic Creator.

What then should be the nature of planning/creativity in the church? It seems obvious to me that if our creativity is to be in sync with the fundamental creating that's going on all around us, it must have a huge element of play in it. Otherwise, we could end up with management procedures indistinguishable from those of business, industry, government and the military, and where does that leave the church? Just one more secular enterprise among many!

EOLITHIC HOMILETICS

Eolithic Creativity is the only way to go. Consider this: Eolithic Creativity is open to, indeed provides a rationale for prayer. Eolithic Creativity keeps those receptors sensitive to incoming messages. Eolithic Creativity keeps us alive, tuned in and turned on. Design does none of this; it has its place, but alone it's downright deadly!

Crafting a sermon is one of those churchy creative procedures. I suspect that most good preachers experience their call week by week as a playful challenge to creativity. The only logical, appropriate and playful title then for this collection of sermons and essays had to be Eolithic Homiletics.

Anyway, if someone asks you about creativity in the church, tell them that sometimes we do things that are irrational even to us, but that turn out all right in the end. Tell them that there are lots of surprises, plenty of mystery, loads of fun and joy. Tell them that love thrives in it, but it's not a very good environment for stress or anxiety. Finally, let them know that it is modeled after God's Creativity. With that you just might offend them.

AUTHORITY:
THEORY & PRACTICE

Over the years that my wife, Lynne and I operated out of Denver, we patronized a certain metro-area church book and supply shop. The main reason that we stayed with them is not that they offered superior service, but because they had no real competition. The problem is that the people we dealt with (whom, basically we liked) worked under such close supervision that there was simply no fun— on either side—in the exchanges that inevitably cropped up. For example, I once noticed a shelf of red and blue leather bound Prayer Books. There was a sign on the red ones, "40% off." Well, I thought, how fortunate, I'd been intending to get one for a gift, but I wanted a blue one. So I went to the clerk. "I notice your personal size prayer books are on sale, (pointing to the shelf). I'd like to buy a blue one—I assume the sale applies to all of them?" "Oh, I don't know," she said nervously, straining to scan the shelf for a clue. "I'll go ask Keith."

Another time I returned a new book in which the binding had fallen apart. I presented it, with receipt, at the counter pointing out the problem, this time to a different clerk, and allowed as how I'd like to exchange it. She studied it apprehensively and concluded, "Oh,

I'll have to go get Keith; he'll have to deal with this." And so it is in this shop when anything out of the ordinary comes up. Consider for a minute the atmosphere in such a workplace. You can feel it almost as soon as you walk in. Or, to put it as a theological question, "What kind of spirit is guiding things in this place?"

I'd like you to contrast that setting with another. I'm going back quite a few years for this one. But it's one of those occasions that become indelibly etched on your mind. The setting was New Jersey. My four year old granddaughter, through some rather careless emergency room attention in a small town hospital ended up comatose and was rushed to a top notch children's ward of a huge hospital in New Jersey's eastern urban strip. They called her condition (she had suffered a momentary heart stoppage) an "insult" to the brain, meaning that the brain cells had not really been destroyed, as with a gunshot wound, but they were "bruised," as when someone receives a sharp blow and swelling ensues. The problem was that the brain has no room for swelling, so such a bruise restricts blood circulation. The treatment was to get the body temperature down, reduce the need for blood, and get the kidneys pumping water out of her system—to reduce the pressure—thus buying time for natural healing to occur. So began a week long vigil, ending with the loss of a granddaughter. That was the occasion.

However, what I wanted to bring to your attention is the way this huge hospital facility, in a violent urban setting, with barred windows, fenced parking lot and under fulltime guard, operated. As a management consultant I continually found myself wondering what kind of management led this huge, tightly secured institution. An illustration: Late one night, having tended to some personal matters, several of us returned to the hospital to pick up on the vigil. I pulled into the nearly empty parking lot and stopped for the guard. He looked us over; "Oh, you're with little Kathi upstairs, aren't you! How is she doing?" Then, "Look, why don't you park over there, and use that entrance," (a much more convenient access than the route normally permitted.) That kind of treatment was experienced over and over during the week. What kind of organization is this where anyone from a parking lot attendant to a nurse's aide seemingly felt entirely free to interpret, bend or suspend the rules as deemed appropriate in special circumstances? Consider the atmosphere in such a workplace. You can feel it almost as soon as you walk in. Or, to repeat the theological question, "What kind of spirit is guiding things in this place?"

Now, to begin to build a theory of authority, I would characterize the actions of personnel in the bookstore as routine, cautious, unimaginative, orderly and dull; the actions of the hospital personnel as loving, risky, creative, free, responsible, and one might add, out of control. In other words (and this is the point), the actions of the bookstore personnel revealed no authority whatever—void, empty; while the actions of the hospital folk were loaded with dynamic, creative authority. In one setting a dearth of authority; in the other a blessed abundance. That's a very sharp contrast, but that's what I experienced. And that contrast should begin to shed some light on how I understand authority. I'll move now toward a more complete definition or theory of authority and then go on to practical considerations for leaders.

Authority is power. Power is the ability to act—to get things done. Authority is power with peculiar qualities. We might call it sanctified power—holy! Authority is that righteous exercise of power that is sanctioned and welcomed by the system. Authority as such, can be contrasted with arbitrary power—coercive or demonic power. In our exercise of ministry in the interest of getting things done—in our work in the world—we doubtless use some mixture of authority as I have characterized it, and coercive power. And I think we know the difference. The actions of the bookstore manager were mostly expressions of coercive power, which, as always drains the entire system of true authority, including the authority of the CEO himself.

Authority is a persistent theme in the Gospel according to Matthew. It comes across in the peculiar way Matthew sets up a scene, or turns a phrase, or departs from Mark or Luke in parallel passages. So, it is, of course Matthew's theory of authority.

There is in Matthew a constant tension between "the authorities"

(Scribes, Pharisees, etc.) who are always maneuvering to protect their appearance of authority and their positions of respect, and are always portrayed as guarding their images. This creates tension between them and Jesus, who, with no position, no office, yet is constantly demonstrating authority. The conflict, of course, is between the standard hierarchical view of authority and something new and strange that the authorities can't fathom and don't want to recognize.

For example, after one of Jesus' healings, the Pharisees scoff, "It is by the power of Beelzebub that he casts out demons." In other words, it must be in the devil's chain of command that he has such power; how else? Jesus counters that it is by the Spirit of God that he has bound the "strong man" (devil) and is thereby free to plunder his house (cast out demons). Again in the temple, Jesus is confronted with "By what authority do you do these things?" And again it is a hierarchical view of authority that lies behind the question. What position, what office, in whose chain of command? And Jesus comes back, "Tell me, the baptism of John, was it of heaven or of men?"

Notice Matthew's twist. The question was not parallel to the one put to Jesus—a question of John's position or office or even of the source of John's authority. The question is a question of John's action (baptism). For Matthew, authority has nothing to do with office, position, title, orders; nothing! Authority is in the action, the deeds. And all true authority is God's authority.

Here is another incident with a strange Matthean twist. Jesus and his followers approach Jerusalem one morning as Jesus, hungry, comes upon a fig tree. But there is no fruit. Jesus cursed the tree and immediately it withered and dried up. If I had been there I'd probably have said, "Gee, why did you do that? It isn't even the season?" But that wouldn't have suited Matthew's staging. So he has the disciples say, "Wow! How did you do that?" There is another form of this incident where the disciples couldn't cast out a demon "because of their little faith." Jesus' response in both cases is the same: "If you had faith you could move this mountain." So we take Matthew's theology of authority a step further: God's authority is manifested in the actions of people of faith. According to Matthew, Jesus has no special authority, and in that, Jesus and his disciples and we, are all equal. The disciples or anyone else might have faith and could be channels of God's authority.

To take another incident: The Baptist is in prison and beginning to lose his original convictions about who this Jesus is. Jesus isn't playing the script quite like John expected. John expected a massage of hellfire and judgment, and Jesus is preaching the Kingdom of Heaven. So John sends his followers to inquire of Jesus, "Are you the one who is to come, or do we look for another?" We might expect Jesus to offer some words of reassurance or explanation, but instead he says, "Go tell John what you see and hear; the blind receive their sight and the lame walk, lepers are cleansed and the deaf hear—and the poor have the good news preached to them." So authority is manifest in acts and words.

Another time Jesus tells his followers, "The Scribes and Pharisees sit on Moses' seat (teach the law with authority); therefore, do whatever they teach you and follow it, but do not do as they do for they do not practice what they preach." So for the true channel of God's authority actions and words are congruent. A similar point is made by Matthew at the close of the Sermon on the Mount where, after a three-chapter long quote of Jesus, Matthew observes, "Now when Jesus had finished saying these things, the crowds were astounded at his teaching, for he taught them as one having authority, and not as one of their Scribes." Note Matthew's not so subtle irony: Jesus (in no position of power) taught with authority—not as "their authorities."

There's more, but let's go with that and sum up Matthew's theory of authority. First, all true authority is God's authority. It has nothing to do with status, corner office, orders or a personal parking place. People in formal "positions of authority" can, and often do, exercise arbitrary power. In fact, the natural tendency of many such people is to take the easy way out, fall back on coercive power and completely miss the meaning of true authority. And in this story that is exactly what happens. The "authorities" never do get it; they finally resort to naked power leading to the crucifixion.

Second, those who are called and respond in faith and in freedom

AUTHORITY: THEORY & PRACTICE

(never coercion) are the channels of God's authority. Jesus is Matthew's prime example, but Matthew constantly reminds the disciples (us) that they (we) can do likewise.

Third, authority is manifest in the actions and the words—which must always be congruent—of people of faith and freedom.

Now, if we accept this theory of authority, what are the implications for leaders?

First, authority is not in limited supply. We have to discard old notions that authority is some kind of "stuff" that we can parcel out or withhold. It is not the case, for example, that I can take some of my authority and parcel it out to someone else in the parish; then I'll have less and he or she will have more. I have no authority. I have no control over authority. It blossoms here and there, in actions and in words, and often unpredictably. But I can't create it! There are some things I can do. I can try to create an environment in which authority flourishes. I can nurture it as one tends a garden. But I have no control over what kind of fruit a particular plant will produce. I can also create a negative environment that smothers true authority. Others in the organization can do that too. If I follow the former course, I too stand a chance of being a channel for God's power. If I follow the latter, none of us will be, for we all smother together under coercive power.

Since authority is not in limited supply, then it follows that (in our parish, for example) there is a gracious abundance of authority blossoming all over the place in ways that often surprise and sometimes delight us. And no one's true authority in any way ever diminishes anyone else's. Where this is not happening, it probably means that some nervous "leader" has a lid on things, as in the bookstore.

It follows then that the leader has to be an incredibly secure person, capable of letting go, accepting the risk, and enjoying the show. I hope that a good theology of authority will encourage such freedom and the enjoyment of seeing the freedom of others, as gifted people of faith, shining forth with God's power. If we understand authority and see how it can be expected to work, perhaps we will find courage

AUTHORITY: THEORY & PRACTICE

to let it work. It does not follow that there is then no system of accountability. It does follow that accountability is not delegated, demanded or coerced. Accountability is elicited of gifted people of faith in freedom called to make a contribution to the community cause.

It is interesting that this "theology" of authority is now being discovered in other sectors of society. Peter Drucker, for example, points out that when progressive companies began rethinking structuring in view of the knowledge revolution, they discovered in retrospect, that the "levels of authority" in the organization chart were no such thing. They were information relays. Where they worked they served to route information effectively—not control. Drucker further observes that one cannot control the knowledge worker. Unlike the old factory worker who relied on the company to provide the means of production—a milling machine, a punch press, etc. the knowledge worker owns his or her means of production— knowledge. "Unless (knowledge workers) know more about their specialty than anyone else in the organization, they are basically useless." So they cannot be "supervised" in the sense of directed or commanded. They can only be accepted as equal members of a team of specialists.

However, there is another side to this. Knowledge workers may be relatively independent and free, but they can't be autonomous. Knowledge workers must have access to an organization where their contribution is accepted. After nearly a lifetime in private practice, I can certainly attest to this. I have enjoyed relative independence, but no one knows better than a "self-employed" specialist how dependant one is on having access to an organization where one can make one's special contribution and experience the satisfaction of doing so. Drucker applies this point both to employees of the organization as well as those with whom the organization contracts for services. We are seeing a growing interdependency among equals and decline of the hierarchy; a development that may be occurring at a greater pace in industry than in the church.

Now, to sum up: behold the hologram (credit card) – the image.

It's as flat as a postcard, yet as you tilt it this way or that, to catch the light from various angles, the image moves, it changes color, and it is-somehow in 3-D. I don't understand the technology involved here, but it is said that the information that constitutes the hologram and our experience of it is not in bits and pieces. It is not like a jigsaw puzzle where, if you lose a couple of pieces you have lost part of the picture. No, in a hologram (so they say) the information that makes the image what it is, is (all of it) stored everywhere. In other words, we could remove any fragment of this image and, if we knew how to do it, recreate the whole image out of the fragment. The whole code is present in any fragment, rather like our whole genetic code is present in every cell in our bodies.

Let us then revisit that hospital in urban New Jersey. This seemed to be a situation in which the whole genetic code that made the hospital what it was, was present in any person who was part of that system. If you dealt with the parking lot attendant, or the janitor, or the head nurse, you experienced yourself dealing with the hospital. And if you got the word from any of the above, you felt that you were getting the word of the hospital, for each spoke as one with authority.

Now imagine a community of Christian people, a congregation where, whatever it is that gives character and identity to that community, is fully present in the actions and words—the ministries—of every member from a five year old child, to a matriarch, to a warden, to a catechumen. Where, when a Sunday visitor meets, or hears the word from any member, or a hungry family picks up a sack of groceries, or a transient gets a tank of gas—whatever—the experience is one of having encountered a community of Christians. They can feel it, almost as soon as they walk in.

Or a hungry family picks up a sack of groceries, or a transient gets a tank of gas—whatever—the experience is one of having encountered a community of Christians. They can feel it, almost as soon as they walk in.

My sisters and brothers, we are collectively and in our various communities back home, members of the Body of Christ. The "genetic code" that makes us one is the fire of the Holy Spirit. And that's the Spirit that rightfully guides things in our company. We have no need or place for arbitrary or coercive power. But let us always delight and rejoice in the phenomenon of God's power finding abundant expression in the gifts and ministries of all God's children. We are not here to smother or control, but to fan the flames and celebrate the miracles.

ADDENDUM: STRUCTURING LOVE

The chair called the meeting to order, opening with a short prayer. She then proposed that, since this was their first meeting, they adopt a few standards to provide for some order for their life together. (She explained that a "standard" was a condition that, once agreed to, all would try to uphold. Standards, to be effective, had to be short, quotable, easily remembered) She proposed for starters, "Meetings start on time." After a very brief discussion, the standard was adopted. A member of the committee offered a second for consideration, "Meetings end on time." The committee was off to a good start. Here is another example of a standard: "If one member thinks it's important, the others at least look at it."

Standards aren't exactly created out of the blue, though it may seem like it at the time. They are derived from values that are likely assumed rather than noticed yet stand over us as a people. Values lack handles and beg interpretation. Standards spell out the details of day to day behavior. "Norms" are standards we unconsciously adopt; they also guide us but we aren't particularly aware of them. There are other terms: regulations, rules, laws, often adopted by someone else and imposed, but also (supposedly) derived from values.

Policy and principals are also derived from the values. However, rather than governing day to day behavior, they guide more basic or longer term decision making. Principals, like norms, might be assumed or unnoticed. We might be inclined to think of them in their manifestation as courtesy, considerateness, protocol. However as necessary, and especially with regard to organizational life, we might be moved to formalize them as policy.

Policy is a formal system of principals. Policy guides decision making, but, again reflects values. The policy of a given system should be internally consistent, understandable and as possible, mutually agreed to. Our Baptismal Covenant is an example of a policy statement. It does not load us up with a lot of rules and regulations. It does not snow us with lofty, undefined ideals. But it does provide a tangible guide.

Word is another term for policy: "I give you my word," "I stand on my word," "You can take my word for it." In each case the term policy can substitute for word. Consider related terms: politics (the process of formulating policy), polity (the structures supporting the process), police (those charged with enforcing policy).

Finally, consider logos; in Greek, the idea, the concept, the primal reality behind the manifest or the existent object. According to Greek thought only the abstract, eternal idea is real. The existing, apparent object is merely a reflection of the eternal reality. Thus, this eternal idea or reality is of God. It is the Word (Logos) of God. "In the beginning was the Word. And the Word was with God, and the Word was God." And the Word became flesh and dwelt among us.

Standards (rules, regulations, etc.) are one layer in a hierarchy of values. We might adopt standards in a committee meeting, but we don't adopt values. We acknowledge values. They precede and stand over us. We are under the judgment of the values that have us! The highest value is Love. Jesus recognized this when asked about the greatest "law." He skipped all the rules and regulations and went straight to the top. Love is the first commandment. There are other values: justice, respect, devotion, dignity. Notice that all these require specification, clarification; they don't stand alone.

What do we mean by justice for instance? Reasonable humans

can consider such matters, discuss and reach agreement by adopting interpretations in the form of standards, laws and so forth. So it is that the law can be considered the structure of love.

The 70 MPH speed limit reflects the value, safety. At one point we saw fit to reduce this to 55 MPH. The new speed limit reflected the value energy conservation. Some claimed that 55 MPH was also safer, but that was incidental; the value under consideration was conservation. (This is an instance where shifting values [safety to conservation] calls for a change in standards [70 to 55 MPH] a likely source of confusion for the public.)

Wherever people of good will gather and attempt to tackle something together they are under the values they are conscious of; or as we say "they are conscientious." However, they might also feel the need to spell out just how the value is to be recognized in this particular case; what kind of behavior will demonstrate observance of the value? Thus, the need for standards. This is what the chair was trying to do; set standards for the committee's life together. Once stated, the values were understood. Things go much better for us when we live in harmony with the values than when we try to proceed at cross purposes with them; so too, with the laws of nature. We can't break the law of gravity, or the laws covering heat transfer, or laws of chemistry. We can only break ourselves in ignoring them. It's to our advantage to understand them and to live under the constraints they represent. So it is with the moral code.

We might understand our journeys through life then as an expression of two hierarchies: a hierarchy of Value and a hierarchy of Purpose. The hierarchy of value governs how we travel; the hierarchy of purpose declares what we are shooting for. In the hierarchy of purpose we wrestle with such questions as: Why are we here? Where are we going? What is my purpose (vocation)? What is/are my call? Goals? Objectives? Targets? The same basic questions apply to a nation, a corporation, a church; questions of intended ends, results, purposes. The hierarchy of purpose is generally considered to be of human origin. We decide who we are and where we are going.

The hierarchy of values however comes first. It precedes us. We acknowledge it as eternal and God given. The top of this hierarchy is Love which John equates with God. Again this hierarchy includes values which beg interpretation. (What do you mean by "justice" in this case? Explain "brotherhood." Who is my "neighbor"?) In an attempt to specify values we come up with principals, policy, and (more detailed) standards, regulations, rules, laws all intended to spell out how the value is to be recognized under specific circumstances.

All this tells us how we are to journey, not where we go! Notice that in a free society "policing" has to do with enforcing the value system. Purposes, goals, vocations and destinations are of no concern to the authorities. If a cop pulls me over on the highway, I can be sure his concern is with how I've been driving, not where I'm going.

Perhaps a diagram will help:

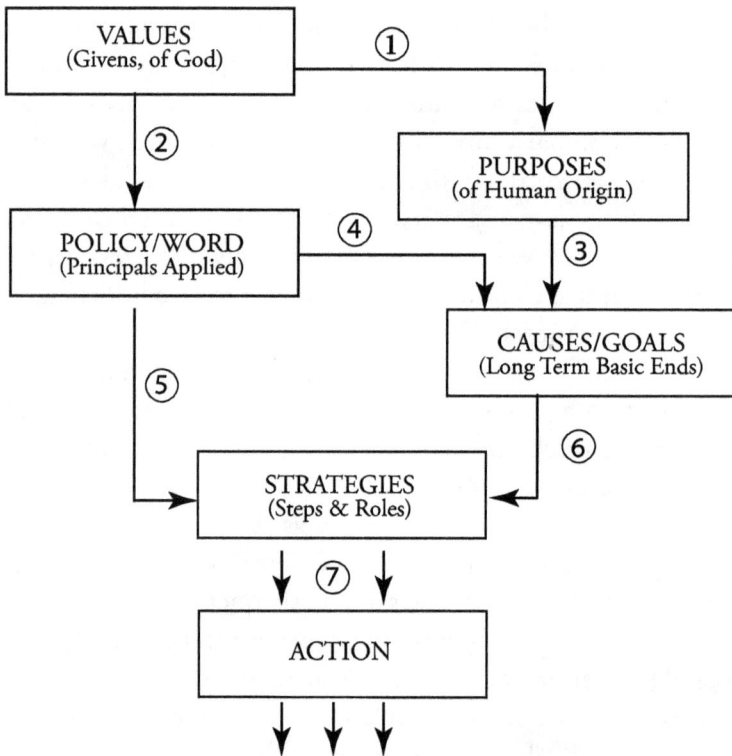

```
  ┌─────────────────┐              
  │   VALUES        │──────①──────┐
  │ (Givens, of God)│             │
  └────────┬────────┘             ▼
           │            ┌──────────────────┐
           ②           │    PURPOSES      │
           ▼            │ (of Human Origin)│
  ┌─────────────────┐   └────────┬─────────┘
  │  POLICY/WORD    │──④──┐      ③
  │(Principals      │     │      │
  │  Applied)       │     ▼      ▼
  └────────┬────────┘   ┌──────────────────┐
           │            │  CAUSES/GOALS    │
           ⑤            │(Long Term Basic  │
           │            │    Ends)         │
           │            └────────┬─────────┘
           │                     ⑥
           ▼                     │
  ┌─────────────────┐            │
  │   STRATEGIES    │◄───────────┘
  │ (Steps & Roles) │
  └──────┬───⑦──────┘
         ▼       ▼
  ┌─────────────────┐
  │     ACTION      │
  └──┬──────┬────┬──┘
     ▼      ▼    ▼
```

However we come by our basic values, for planning purposes, we might as well say they are givens. However they got in place, they are our starting point. From these values we (1) come to a sense of vocation or purpose in life. We are here for a reason. We also arrive at (2) certain principals which will likely guide us throughout our life's journey. With that, the basics of life are in place: what we are up to and how we will travel the road; and we find that there is meaning in life (The hierarchy of values on the left) and purpose (The hierarchy of purpose on the right)

From here we are ready to determine our fundamental aims in life (3); choices which are strongly influenced by the principals already in place (4). And from there we can plot a series of activities to get us there (6), plans also strongly influenced by established principals (5). All of which takes us to a course of action intended to achieve the desired results. (7) This is our "Structure of Love."

FN: Patte, Daniel, The Gospel According to Matthew, Fortress Press

PROPERTIES OF LEADERSHIP

Consider for a moment a tripod; the tripod supporting your organization identifying purpose, maintaining health, creating teamwork. Being a tripod, it's essential that it have three sound legs. Otherwise it's not a tripod.

The three legs of leadership are management, authority and care. It takes a certain interdependent configuration of three to retain the idea "tripod." It is possible to think of management, authority and care singly, but in so doing, each is distorted. Their true qualities are only appreciated insofar as we can see them in their tripodal unity: leadership. Got a mental picture of that in your mind's eye?

Now picture that tripod with one or two legs missing, or trying to function on one or two legs at a time, or with all three legs bent, twisted or broken. Purpose, vision, energy; in short, leadership has vanished. So have authentic management, authority and care.

Management is the acceptance of accountability for results in some defined or understood area of endeavor, and the acceptance of accountability to someone else. Note the two parts: responsibility for results; accountability to another. The church's term for management is stewardship. When the word stewardship is used it reminds us that, bottom line, accountability is to God. When the word management is used, the implied context is usually organizational. But there is really no essential difference between the two concepts. The definition fits both.

Authority is power sanctified—recognized and accepted—by the system; power exercised with systemic approval and blessing, thus made legitimate. Power is the ability to act. So considered power is essentially good. No one should be powerless; everyone should be empowered to take part in the affairs of society, although, of course, people may use power in good or evil ways. Inherent personal gifts may be turned into authority in formal ways, such as electing or appointing someone to a position of responsibility, and in informal ways, such as patriarchs and matriarchs of a small congregation. However, there is no real power in the person or position, only in the action. Authority has no reality in the abstract, only in the living.

Care is looking after one another as in tough love; dogged, determined attention. It is an expression of love and of acknowledgement of our interdependence and mutual responsibility for the welfare of the whole.

Finally, leadership as we are considering it, is the union of management, authority and care. It is important to emphasize union. While management, authority and care could be thought of as rightful aspects of leadership, the point is that the three stand together; three properties of a single reality. Management, authority and care are, in essence one. Any one of these essential components disassociated from the others tends toward distortion and true leadership is lost. Any one practiced without regard for the others loses its essential character and the action itself is a travesty of the original intent. The quality and depth are lost, for the qualities of one include the force and influence of the others. Without management, authority and care in dynamic, creative union the action cannot be called leadership.

True management then, includes the qualities of love, authority and accountability. Torn loose from its ontological partners, it tends to spin off into shallow, pragmatic efficiency and the ruthless pursuit of selfish ends. The sense of accountability to higher powers and authorities is lost, and responsible stewardship is reduced to crass manipulation.

True authority includes the qualities of loving concern for others, a sense of awe of power; a sense of justice and fairness for all. Separated from its base in reality, it will likely spin off into giddy glorifying of naked power, an irresponsible, uncaring exercise of clout for the sheer warped joy of it. Accountability is an unneeded burden.

True care includes the qualities of justice, authority and stewardship; responsible management of resources. Unhooked from its ontological roots, it spins off into emotional, irresponsible tolerance of everything posing as "love;" anything goes. All sense of accountability is sacrificed and true pastoral concern is lost.

Management and authority void of care has lost agape and the drive for unity, quality and effectiveness. The action is hard, calculating, legalistic, task oriented; there is no grace in the action.

Authority and care void of management has lost accountability and the need for unity, quality and effectiveness. All that's left is a warm glow plus good feelings and intentions. There is no creativity in the action.

Care and management void of authority has lost credibility and the possibility of unity, quality and effectiveness. There is good will in the intention but no energy in the action.

True leadership includes the need, the drive and the hope for quality effectiveness and it expresses grace, creativity and energy in the action. With any combination of the above distortions, vision and purpose are lost. The organization is rudderless, non-credible, immoral—or all three. There is no leadership; the essence of it has evaporated.

We have been dealing with concepts. Let us now shift to practices; from management to manager, from leadership to leader, from the concept to the bearer and performer. The leader is a manager with authority. It is the leader who must be integrated. It is not sufficient that we should seek a balance in management, authority and care in one's practice of leadership as though one intended to give each its fair share of attention or as though each were a role one played out in turn or a "hat" one wore on particular occasions as needed while the other two were momentarily suspended. Those qualities must be integrated into a single performance of leadership. Nor is it sufficient that each property be reduced to a consideration to be factored into each judgment so that each decision is a compromise.

The absence of the quality of management in a leader's performance is irresponsibility. The absence of authority is abdication. The absence of care is apathy. A compromise involving irresponsibility, abdication and apathy is certainly not leadership.

What is desired is that the leader be leader and that the actions exhibit leadership. What is desired in the practice of leadership is that management, authority and care be so integrated that what is practiced is leadership, not a self-conscious temporary role or function. When this is the case the leader is scarcely aware in a given act, whether it comes out of pastoral or managerial concerns. The question is usually meaningless to the effective leader whose focus is to do what is right, not managerially or pastorally correct, nor merely a demonstration of power. In taking the best action, all qualities of leadership will usually be well served.

Let's take a look at a real life example and see how these points might play through. Joe Brown has been ordained 15 years. Early on he covered several short term parochial positions. He has been rector of Heavenly Rest for 10 years. No one quite recalls why he was called, but most members long ago came to the conclusion that he should never have been ordained, let alone called to Heavenly Rest. Joe's passion is automobiles. He has done well in recent stock car derbies and is proud of his customized, souped-up Chevy. The people actually like him as a person and they like his wife, who has a flair for hospitality and sensitivity to people. But Joe is inept and apathetic as a parish priest. Some of the guys in the men's club are feeling a bit guilty these days. One had suggested that Joe was using the parish as an economic base to support his car hobby. Others quickly agreed. Now, the guilt. After all, "judge not!" So the parish muddles through, sort of. Some discouraged families have dropped out. Attendance has declined and the budget is not keeping up with inflation. There is just no fun or inspiration in being part of Heavenly Rest any more. Things are not quite bad enough for the vestry to take action. But the parish has lost its best leadership. Prognosis: the decline will continue until it takes nearly all the income to support the rector; then there will be some kind of a crisis. Joe will be out and the church will be a wreck; give it maybe another two years.

The recently retired bishop knew about Heavenly Rest. However, looking forward to retirement, there seemed no point in getting into a fracas that he might not have time to resolve, so he lived with it. The new bishop, being a local person, also knows about the situation. So, the question now is what is the best course of action for the new bishop? We can look at some options.

Option A: Do nothing, it's a local problem. Let the local folk deal with it. Besides, maybe it will go away.

Analysis: Since the authority is in the action, not the position, and since there is no action, there is no authority. The bishop is, and probably feels, powerless. This option is called abdication. The earlier prognosis stands.

Option B: Out of pastoral concern for Joe, the bishop calls him into his office for a friendly chat. After exchanging pleasantries and getting some acknowledgement from Joe that things have not been going well, the bishop, determined to be firm, closes by saying that things simply have to improve, and to assure that they do, the two will meet once a month to consult and review progress. Meantime, assuming that there are signs of improvement, the matter will be strictly between the two of them.

Analysis: In this case the bishop has at least assumed some responsibility. However the plan will not work—not in a situation that has been developing for 10 years. Besides it is a denial of the apparent problem. It is also a denial of the essence of leadership. One leg of the tripod is missing; management. So things will merely drift through further concessions, promises and mild threats. Prognosis: same as before.

Option C: Feeling the weight of managerial responsibility, the bishop calls Joe and the wardens of Heavenly Rest into his office. After a brief review of the situation, they all come to an agreement that within six months Joe will find new employment. Then (remembering his pastoral "hat") the bishop promises full support and assistance in helping Joe get something lined up.

Analysis: Again, the bishop has at least acted. He's having a little trouble keeping track of hats, but he's on the move. However, the strategy reeks of compromise. Prognosis: It is nearly 100 percent predictable that (1) when the six months are up, Joe will need "just a little more time." This and subsequent extensions will push the six months to at least 12, at which point Joe will really start looking for a job but will need the rectory for a couple more months so he can line up a move. (2) During this period of time Joe will start bad-mouthing the diocese, the national church and who knows what else? Thus a vocal minority will be created in Heavenly Rest, singing the chorus, "Ain't it awful the way the bishop treated poor Joe?"

The wounds and divisions created will seriously hamper the next calling process. Also, it's at least 50 percent predictable that pressure on the bishop and a bishop's uncanny ability to see redeeming qualities in nearly everyone will contribute to the bishop misleading a colleague, and he will be a party to transferring a problem to another diocese rather than resolving it.

Option D: Seeing that things are deteriorating fast and that decisive action is called for, the bishop calls Joe into his office. The mood is serious, characterized by mutual respect, and the two deal with facts that the bishop has assembled. After reviewing the situation, including a hard look at the question of Joe's call to a church vocation, the bishop informs Joe that he expects his resignation within a week and that he vacate the rectory within a month. (Joe has one more Sunday with the congregation.) And, with Joe's cooperation the bishop will cover the costs of quality career counseling service and insist that Heavenly Rest provide Joe with a four-month sabbatical in addition to whatever vacation time is due. Failing Joe's cooperation, the bishop will meet with the Heavenly Rest vestry and propose that they initiate formal procedures for the dissolution of a pastoral relationship. Furthermore, if it has to come to that, the bishop will guarantee nothing regarding termination benefits beyond what is formally due.

Analysis: This is a confrontation that allows Joe no weasel room. He must finally deal with realities. Yet, it still preserves his self-respect. There is nothing dishonorable in resigning a job and taking a little time to reconsider one's call. After all, Joe hasn't been "fired" (at least not publically) and can explain his actions any way he wishes. No point in the bishop denying him that. Joe hasn't been accused of any criminal activity. The action also frees the parish to get on with its life in short order.

In Option C we predicted that Joe would turn against the system, given the opportunity. Yet here we propose giving him one more Sunday with the congregation. Is this inconsistent? No! It's a different set of circumstances. Under Option C, Joe is under the gun and everyone knows he's in trouble. His better qualities might make it possible for him to "take it like a man" for a week or so, but it would take a saint to get through six months. Sooner or later an ordinary human must begin to mentally rework things to put oneself in a better light; then the defensive tactics begin. It is simply not fair to expect someone to get through such a trial period without lashing back. It's certainly not the pastoral thing to do.

On the other hand, giving him one Sunday under Option D provides the opportunity for healthy termination of the relationship. Joe can explain his plans, recall good times, confess shortcomings, express gratitude, tell a joke and say goodbye—any combination. And greetings, laughs and tears can be exchanged at the coffee hour. Closure is accomplished. There is, of course, the slight possibility that Joe will use the occasion to blame the bishop and others, and make himself out to be the victim. Should he take this unlikely course, he's gone Monday anyway and as the congregation reflects on the performance, they will be grateful for a bishop who had it right all along and who acted. Closure complete anyway.

Is the four month sabbatical overly generous? No, it's probably sufficient under the circumstances, but, remember the church is a party to the problem. Joe isn't totally to blame. The congregation let the situation drift for a long time and so must assume some moral responsibility. In any case, Option C would have cost a very minimum of six months compensation while conditions continued to deteriorate.

Prognosis, Option D: Joe will probably cooperate once he sees that the bishop is firm and remembers his own position in the parish is pretty weak. He might negotiate details. For example, maybe he is not interested in career counseling; maybe he'd rather use that money toward a course in automobile mechanics or to purchases a newer model Chevy. If he is foolish enough to reject the offer outright, the bishop proceeds as promised. The whole matter will likely be resolved sooner than under any other option considered.

Option D appears to be the best way to go. It treats Joe with maximum honesty, integrity and dignity and (however he responds) gets him in touch with reality the fastest. It offers the least turmoil in the life of the congregation while placing them on a firm foundation for pursuing a new search process. In short, Option D best serves the three legs of the leadership tripod; management, authority and care. Yet, we didn't get to it by compromising the three properties of leadership, but by asking "What is best?" and responding out of a unity called "leadership."

We can dig a little deeper into this dynamic of wholesome human relationships and examine the more basic realities. Paul Tillich does this in a little book called Love, Power and Justice. According to Tillich, for God, love, power and justice is a single reality. We could say that essentially, or, in essence, love, power and justice is one. So considered, it is meaningless to talk of any one of them singly, or in a way that suggests possible trade-offs. For example, I can't suspend love for a moment while I mete out justice in a given situation. Nor can I overlook justice in the name of loving concern. Nor can I claim to be acting in the name of either while I withhold power.

Each of the three belongs to the other two. No one standing alone means what we usually think it means. Each contributes important qualities to the others. Love by itself is sweet, syrupy emotion. Power alone is an arbitrary, random explosion of energy. Justice gone solo isn't much more than book balancing. The three belong together in effective unity. By itself each loses the rich depth and value we believe rightfully belong to each.

However existentially, for us in the here and now, each constantly struggles to be treated singly. Our tendency is indeed to see trade-offs and compromises. Love, power and justice are three realities each to be served in turn. So it is that in the name of love I might be found tolerant of some injustice. "Yes, we can let it go this time, he's our brother!" Or, in the name of justice, compromise love; "He had it coming!" Or, giddy with power, slight both love and justice,;"My country, right or wrong." There are countless ways of ignoring one property while focused on another.

And such is the case with leadership; the essence of leadership is management, authority and care in dynamic, creative union. Attempts to honor any one of them without regard to the others will inevitably distort the one to the point of making it meaningless, and it will destroy true leadership. Yet the key to leadership is to not honor any one of them singly, but to perform as leader while the union, the single reality, of management-authority-care is honored. In leadership terms this is the direct parallel of Tillich's love-power-justice.

The question then becomes, how does one called to a leadership position become the kind of person required to function as an effective leader with regard to the qualities of leadership we have been considering here? What is required in the leader is courage. Courage is related to being. One is not except with courage. It is quite similar to authority. There is no authority except in the act. Courage initially is self-affirmation, saying "yes" to one's own being. It is self-affirmation in spite of fear and anxiety: fear of guilt, anxiety rooted in threat of non-being. Self-acceptance and hence courage is rooted in the faith of being accepted. Thus, courage is ultimately affirmation of God.

Christians of all people should be courageous because Christians know that the price of guilt has been paid in the cross and that all actions are redeemable. Fear and anxiety for the leader contemplating an action is also influenced by the truth that the contemplated act is risky and the leader is probably not confident that all the facts are readily at hand. The leader might well be blessed with a good grasp of leadership, but not have the courage of his/her convictions. It takes courage to act even when the intuitions are good and the proposed action is the best possible. It takes some courage on the part of the surgeon to take scalpel in hand and start. Courage takes the threat of risk into itself.

It may be even with good intentions and lots of self-confidence there is still some element of doubt. No matter how expert the operator, there must always be some question of whether the data are sufficient in detail or entirely accurate. So courage must take the threat of ignorance into itself. The leader is not a computer capable of cranking out precise answers to the tenth decimal place, nor is the information input 100 percent of what might be desired. The alternative however, is no action and that's not leadership. The third steward was "cast into outer darkness," not because he was a man of modest ability (his ability was affirmed in the giving of the one talent), but because he wouldn't risk what he had. His choice was non-being, "outer darkness."

So, it appears that all leaders are faced with some threat of doubt, ignorance and guilt (And I'd be afraid of a leader not feeling some of this.), and consequently in need of wisdom and the courage to affirm oneself, take hold and take action. Therefore one doesn't routinely work solo but does routinely seek guidance from the Lord. One might have a few trusted colleagues and confidants at hand—a place to test ideas, bounce them around, see what they sound like rebounding from another mind. The hope is to improve overall the wisdom going into decision making. Not that the leader must consult with someone else before making any decision—that would be crippling and demeaning—but that one keeps in touch with others as a general rule; sharing doubts, reflecting together on pending issues and on actions already taken. The point is to improve overall performance; to learn and to grow, not assure that every action is above scrutiny or perfect. One cannot expect to never make a mistake unless one is prepared to do nothing. There will be some risk and some doubt except where there is no agenda. But one needs the courage to accept the doubt and take the risk. Wisdom and confidence are keys to courage. Courage is the key to action. Action rooted in a well-integrated base of management, authority and care is leadership. And leadership is the foundation of the organization.

DEVELOPING THE PARISH BASE

"Preaching is conversation but it is serious conversation; two persons (or a preacher and congregation) with enough in common to be able to communicate, with enough difference to need to communicate, and each with an open willingness to be influenced by the other."

— Fred B. Craddock; Collected Sermons; Introduction

A) AUTHORITY

Will you proclaim by word and example the Good News of God in Christ?

...I will, with God's help.

That is out of our Baptismal Covenant. One doesn't need to be ordained to preach. A baptized person is **expected** to proclaim "by word and example" the Gospel; but not in isolation.

Will you who witness these vows do all in your power to support this person in (his) life in Christ?

...We will.

This is a **community** pledge as well. . So it is with all parochially based ministries. The local church is the support base for the ministries of her members in world and church; this can be the reality where it is consciously pursued. If it is not the case, lay preaching is not likely to be accepted. The people will believe they are being cheated. Some years ago I had the privilege of developing such a parochial base where everybody's ministry was appreciated, and experienced how rich it can be. Here are some vignettes to illustrate:

As rector of the church and at their request I met with leaders of our Stephen Ministry program. They were laying plans for the training of new recruits and needed to clear certain dates. At one point, one of them turned to me and announced, "Now, on (a particular Sunday) we want a sermon on the caring ministry of all Christians." I must have looked blank, so she shot back, "You got a problem with that?" I hurried to pick it up. "Oh no, it's just that I was trying to remember; I think that's the Sunday Sherri is scheduled to preach." Without hesitation she answered, "That's okay, we don't care who preaches, but we want a sermon on caring ministries."

We had put in a new sound system. Fifteen year old Paul was made our sound technician. So he sits at the board, turns the knobs, pulls the levers, etc. As things worked out I didn't have occasion to use it the first few Sundays it was in place. Then it was Christmas Eve and I would be wearing the battery pack and the tiny, clip-on mike. So I went to Paul and asked, "Now, will you brief me on how this thing works?" Paul looked up at me from the console, "Oh, are you preaching tonight?"

The husky man's voice on the other end of the line, after introducing himself, said, "I'm trying to get a message to Eric Johnson. Eric is my mother's minister." (I knew the caller; He's a farmer out east of town, and his mother is in a local nursing home.) So I said, "Oh yes, I know how to reach Eric Johnson. If you want to give me the message, I'll see that he gets it." It turned out that his mother had been temporally removed to a hospital. So the Johnsons and I made hospital calls. Eric and Diana Johnson were two of our Eucharistic ministers. They had been ministering to Edith over the previous three years.

So the context for lay preaching is an environment in which everyone's baptismal ministry is affirmed, supported and appreciated. That's the basis of the authority to preach. It simply has to be experienced as normative in the ongoing life of the community. But that prompts another question; are people expected to be licensed before they preach? If so, how can they try themselves and how does the congregation know whom to call as preachers? That, in turn raises another query. Does the license confer authority, or recognize authority? The answer seems obvious: It recognizes authority already there. I've already shown that congregational sanction of the ministry is the basis of authority.

We developed our ministry of preaching when our diocese had no provision for licensing the canonical lay ministries. At that point it was no issue. Later on, the diocese did adopt provisions for formally licensing the canonical lay ministries and we went through the motions of trying to comply. It soon became obvious that the group charged with this responsibility on behalf of the diocese had no background or sense of what we were up to. So we had to skip diocesan licensing policy and proceed on our own course. It made no difference to our membership and no one else bothered us. However, it seemed to demonstrate that diocesan licensing is a cumbersome and unneeded step in "authorizing" this ministry.

B) PREPARATION

Preaching must be taught. In the church referenced above, education had been a high priority for many years. Many of our folk were graduates or students of Education for Ministry (EFM), a four year intensive seminary extension course. Some were Stephen Ministers. We never missed a chance to send people out for special training events beyond the parish. In other words we were a highly educated "community in ministry" (as distinct from a "community gathered around a minister"). Training for all aspects of ministry was considered normal. The point is, in designing our training for preaching we could concentrate on preaching and assume a basic theological literacy was in place.

The setting for our initial training was a weekly series of brown bag lunches. That practice continued for many years as monthly luncheons. In preparation for these meetings I would type out brief quotations from scripture on slips of paper and place them, face down, on the center of the table. Each participant then selected a slip at random and that was their text for the exercise. I did not select obscure quotes; the point was not to stump them but to get them started. As we continued with our lunch, each preacher would get up, speak for one minute and sat down. This is not an easy task. But performance improved rapidly. Initially they would start out, slip in hand, reading their quote then commenting on it (Deductive preaching; see twelve considerations, ahead.), and they would be quite awkward in closing. (Opening and closing; see twelve considerations, ahead.) However, with practice and training, performance improved rapidly. They could stand without props, speak confidently and sit without embarrassment.

At one of our luncheon sessions, a gentleman, well educated in the basics of the faith and now testing his call to preach, stood up but couldn't find words to start. He stood there embarrassed, stumped, others waiting. One of the women said; "It's okay, Burette, we all love you." It struck me right then and there, that this was one of the essentials. Knowing that they love you, that they're on your side, rooting for you, is a huge part of the license to go. It worked for Burette.

At another of our luncheon sessions we came up with this exercise: Each preacher was asked to outline a generic sermon on paper; never mind the content, just an outline of the several moves that they might normally come up with in crafting any sermon. They had no problem understanding the task. Here are three examples:

See twelve considerations (No. 9) Crafting

I	Attention Getter	Collect the tools	Set Up
II	My point	Set them up	The Case
III	Getting at it	Paint bold strokes	Illustration/ Example
IV	Tying it all together	Paint in details	Pull it all together
V		Hang the picture	Punch Line

For a congregation just starting a lay preaching program, I'd suggest starting with a small group of preachers, not one. It's too much to put on one person who is then too visible before the whole church. Announce their meetings publically so the congregation is aware of what is going on. Invite others in. However don't publish a list of preaching assignments in advance. Don't make it a popularity contest. Preachers appear as scheduled with no 'to-do' list just like readers and ushers. Then lay preaching is accepted as normal.

C) SPINNING YARNS

What is the difference between laughter in response to a joke and the "ah ha" experience in response to a parable or story? Not much, really. In both cases, it's the surprise twist at the end that grabs attention. A joke however gives rise to amusement—a short term payoff. A good story provokes insight—a long term payoff. That's why many people have trouble remembering jokes; the payoff is so short term.

One of the details that make a story is what I call "set up." To pull off a good story one must see how setup works. There is usually a key word or phrase that sets up the listener for the punch line. If one doesn't get that part in place at the proper point, the story doesn't come off. See the tale, "Miracle on the Sisseton," later in this book. The setting is a large Lakota Convocation on a reservation in South Dakota. In this story a white priest addresses the gathering apologetically (some arrangements had been overlooked) and remarks jokingly, "I guess the committee failed to function." The joke flops. Later in the story a Native American stands to give his report on this same committee. His report is modest, humble. The end of the story sneaks up on the listener who finally realizes, almost as a double take, the miracle that came out of the committee that failed to function. If the storyteller fails to set up the listeners early on with the quote from the priest, the sense of irony is lost and the story has no punch.

There is a story, "Red Flowers" that is used regularly in workshops that has a phrase, "It was red, with a green stem." The phrase occurs several times—twice amusingly, the third time, devastatingly. Without the repetition the third rendering would be limp. There's another story, "The King's Magnificent Team," in which the performance of two teams is described. In this case it is the repetition in the description of the two teams that sets up the case. Understanding how the story works certainly contributes to effective story telling; it also helps one remember the detail. We have many stories on file we use in workshops and they all have titles for our convenience in planning things. We do not use titles in introducing or telling stories however. Just tell them! Introducing a story by title is not a good set up.

Another characteristic of most good stories is specificity of detail: names, places, times etc, as appropriate to the story. Garrison Keillor is a master at this. Listen to his yarns. Think of how they would come off if he got lazy with detail. "This guy stopped in for a drink," versus "Wally dropped into the Side Track Tap for a beer and a bump." Detail helps the listener get a mental picture of what is going on. The story comes alive. Keillor is tops in providing chuckles as he builds for a poignant close.

Parables on the other hand seem to work well without a lot of detail. "A certain man had two sons. One day the younger son came to his father . . ." Keillor, in his version of the visit of the magi, adds a lot of flourishes—one of the visitors, he speculates, was Lutheran—a serious myth becomes a humorous yarn. Specificity and detail are worth paying attention to. Design the story well; tell it well, then let it stand on its own. Don't explain it. If it's a good story, someone might hear something you didn't think of. It happens all the time. The Evangelists sometimes felt compelled to "explain" Jesus' parables, but most scholars believe that Jesus did not. He popped them in and let them go.

D) TWELVE CONSIDERATIONS FOR PREACHERS

1. The Text: The readings assigned for the day are the most obvious source. However there are others: the creed, the Decalogue, the liturgy, the collect, theological or seasonal themes, etc. There is usually a common theme in the collective readings of the day, and since the theme generally carries through all three years of the lectionary cycle it may be apparent in the collect for the day. Focus however is crucial. Don't try to cover everything. One might focus on one primary text and bring others in to support or illustrate. But if the text is Mark, let Mark come through; don't blend all the gospels into one generic gospel.

2) The situation: What is going on in the world; the congregation? What are people thinking about, talking or concerned about? In preparation one might start with a preview of the readings for the day and their message, then mentally lay them alongside the headlines of the recent week. Where do they touch each other? The sermon is part of a dialogue. What is on the world's end of that conversation? "No word is the word of God unless it is the word of God for someone." (Tillich)

3) The Aim: If one intends to teach, inform, explain, the objective is an educated community. If one is probing social or moral issues, the objective is help in thinking things through, not providing "correct" or "final" answers. If it is prophesying (telling it as it is), the objective is response/action. "Some sermons aim to comfort the afflicted, some to afflict the comfortable." However, all should build up and nurture community, not tear it apart.

4) **The Approach:** Exegesis is studying the text to discern the message on its own terms. Exposition is studying the text to get at the message as it applies to us. Theme building is following a theme ("bread," "sin," "walking," etc.) through several passages or Sundays or a season. Displacement is "putting on" another culture or time to experience it from the inside: "You are a teenager in Palestine in about 60 CE." These categories are not mutually exclusive.

5) **Sequencing:** Deductive preaching is starting with the text and developing the message. Inductive preaching is starting with something else (perhaps totally unrelated on first view) and developing it to the point where the text can be introduced then heard in a fresh new way.

6) **The Target:** If the target is the head, the sermon will be "intellectual." If the target is the heart the sermon will be "emotional." If the target is the intuition, the sermon will be "open-ended." Seek a balance. If the message is merely intellectual, there will be no soul. If it is merely emotional, there will be no substance. If it is not somewhat open-ended, it will be finished—nothing for the folk to ponder afterward. And this: "If the sermon goes over their heads, it doesn't mean that you are brighter; it means you are a poor shot."

7) **The Stories:** There is THE STORY and our stories. Our stories are all part of THE STORY. The sermon can help people understand and appreciate this. Creation, exodus, captivity, incarnation, baptism, crucifixion, resurrection, Pentecost, etc. run through all stories. "It's the people telling their stories that gives the Gospel its wings to fly." (African Bishop Kivengere)

8) **Breadth and Variety:** As with eating, people need wholesome balance. Constantly aiming for the same target, or preaching the same theme won't get it. "In our parish, no matter what the lessons, we get the same sermon." (A parishioner; another parish of course.)

9) **Crafting:** A sermon that rambles all over the map for 20 minutes will not communicate. There should be a clear sequence of moves—say three to five—very consciously delivered in order. The preacher should be very clear about what is to be accomplished in each move then aim for that result, get it, then go on to the next,

building the overall case. The attention span of the congregation is quite up to handling a well-ordered series of moves, one at a time, but not a 20-minute muddle. If the structure is well handled, the congregation will not be particularly conscious of it, but will know that the case is moving along.

10) **Openings and Closings:** These have to be carefully planned. A good opening captures attention and gives the preacher a license to go on. A good closing powerfully caps, summarizes or concludes the message and gives the preacher leave to sit down. Don't close with a "Thank You." (If "thanks" are due it should go the other way.) And don't end with a feeble "Er—ah—um—well I guess that's it." Often a good closing is like a punch line of a joke; there is a twist that isn't exactly expected, but with it, the whole sermon comes into focus.

11) **Preacher is Human:** The sermon is not an occasion to dump personal baggage all over the congregation, but to speak God's Word. Still the preacher is a person and the communication is person to person.

12) **Purposes:** Bottom line, what is the purpose? John puts it this way:

"There are many other signs that Jesus did. If all were to be written down, the whole world couldn't contain the books that would be written, but these are written that you may believe that Jesus is the Christ, the Son of God, and that believing you may have life in his name."

In that context, what is the purpose of this particular sermon?

(Some of the quotes above are old proverbs for preachers. I can't claim authorship but want to tag them as reminders.)

E) HOLY AND SACRAMENTAL

Many years ago I was working with a group of youngsters on confirmation instruction when we got into a serious discussion on the meaning of the word holy. There was one young lady in the group, age ten or eleven, who was the eldest of five kids in her family. Her parents had to work hard at the family business to keep that operation going, and this little girl, like so many 'oldest children' had a sense of responsibility well beyond her years; looking after younger siblings, taking care of the house in her parents' absence, and her involvement with the Lord and his church was a very important part of all this.

We were struggling to share our sense of the meaning of the word holy when I saw her eyes light up and she said, "Father Wilson, I know what holy means." I nodded to coax her along. "Holy is like when your mother," she spoke slowly and deliberately, her voice quiet and mysterious, "Holy is like when your mother makes a birthday cake and decorates it, and it's so beautiful—you don't want to cut it." I remembered a clergy conference some years earlier, sitting at the feet of Bishop Angus Dunn, as he struggled with the same question. "Holy," he had said, "is that upon which one dare not impose oneself."

"Yes," I whispered to the group, "That's what holy is."

But we do cut the cake—and share it—and eat it. Otherwise, what's the point? We do impose ourselves; on the cake, on the church, on each other. We dare to taste, to touch, to feel that which is holy. We are sensual, physical, carnal! Yet we are holy; we are (shall we say) sacramental! Sacramental is the capacity to experience the spiritual in and through the physical of our own reality and that of our environment. We live in both worlds; a world we can see, feel, smell, hear and taste, and a world we perceive in some extrasensory manner but which is nevertheless as real.

Those of us called to preach the Word live in this world and we attempt to speak God's word to people who live in this same world. That ministry of speaking God's Word is in its own right a Sacrament. Preaching is a spiritual connection and communication among souls via tongue and ear over which God's Grace is experienced in God's Creation. Yes, yes, that's what preaching is!

PART TWO

SERMONS AND Themes

FROM THE BEGINNING

In the beginning the earth was without form and void. That is, there was no structure, no matter, no purpose—well, when you get right down to it, there just wasn't anything at all. Then one day (before there were days) God, in a reflective mood, said, "I think it'd be really cool if we had something around here instead of nothing." He pondered this idea for a little eternal while, and said, "Let it Be!"

The power of his Word went forth to carry out what the word ordered. Then followed a hundred zillion hydrogen explosions; heat, light, cosmic dust—swirling, spinning, gathering itself into huge orbits of matter; spheres charging, creating space as they hurtled around each other. Dust cooled, steam condensed into water, mountains and streams formed, moons, planets and stars appeared in patterns in the sky. And with all this, time took its first tentative steps.

All creation praised the Lord. The mountains witnessed to God's majesty. The streams sang his praises. The stars in the heavens glorified his Holy Name. And God looked out over it all and said, "Wow, that's pretty good!"

The power of God's Word sustained the changing, growing creation and the ages unfolded. Then God said, "Yes, it is good, but we should have more color and self-driven change and the power of renewal season by season. Clearly that means that 'life' must be part of creation." So, again He said, "Let it Be!"

And again the power of God's Word went forth to do that which the Word commanded. The whole earth burst into color; green leaves, ferns, trees all over the place; flowers of every imaginable hue and shade, growing, always fresh and new, replenishing themselves continually, reacting to the elements. There were daisies and giant redwoods, thistles and ponderosa pines, pin oaks and white oaks and red oaks, spinach and poison ivy, orchids, lilies and violets, cactuses and tumbleweed.

And the moss on the rock in the swamp and the Douglas fir reaching to the heavens and the sagebrush and the dandelion praised the Holy name of God. And God watched all—saw the sustaining power of his Word throughout—and God said, "Hey, that is good!"

Eons rolled by, season followed season, and God's creation endured through time in the midst of the void, sustained by his Word. Then God said, "But there isn't really much action in all this. My Spirit is far too restless for such a dull creation. There simply must be more playful and random mobility and interesting activity." God smiled at the thought and once again called forth: "Let it Be!"

And once again the power of his Word exploded in compliance. And the world was filled with every kind of running, crawling, flying, swimming, jumping; yelling, whistling, roaring, yelping, barking, chirping critter imaginable. They were all colors: pink, red, brown, yellow; some were multi-colored and some even changed color. They were covered with fur, feather or scale, growing and replenishing themselves, changing and interacting with one another. There were the whale and rhinoceros, the hippopotamus, the kangaroo and the grasshopper, the ladybug, swallow and dinosaur, the mosquito and the great Arabian stallion. There were puppy dogs and white faced calves, turtles and bobcats, eagles and armadillos. And to the glory of God, and in praise of His Holy name, they scampered, galloped, darted and soared. And God looked and said, "Ahh, that is good indeed!"

FROM THE BEGINNING

The ages rolled on and God's creation continued churning out time before the void, driven by the force of his Word; birth, death, evolution, changing patterns, existence out of essence, creation out of chaos in the midst of eternity, molding, sustaining, supporting, coaxing, urging, energizing creation's bold movement toward ultimate reality.

And God said, "There's one more detail to cover. No one knows I've been creatin'. I'll make one more critter, a little like the animals—a part of creation—but a little like me, with self awareness. A creature who will see that I've been creatin', who can know and appreciate, who can help it continue in accordance with its own character, not just my ideas. One to be free, not to glorify me stupidly and automatically, but who can decide." Then, God continued, "I will make him out of dust so he will always know what he is, and I will call him adam (God's word for dust)." And God said, "Let it be."

God's word shot forth to carry out that which the word ordered. And there stood Adam. The creature looked around, dazed but self-conscious and said, "Somebody's been creatin'!! Wonder if it was me?" (We always do get those roles mixed up!) Then, "No, I think I'm part of it!" And God said, "Ah, yes, this is very good!"

Adam stood on the shore of the sea, saw the might of the wind, the waves and the tide, saw that they were a glory to their creator. He saw the vast expanse of God's creation and felt very small, and a chill ran up his spine. He also saw, in his dim, dawning awareness, that his very ability to experience his own insignificance was a clue to his greatness.

Then he stood on top of the mountain; saw the glory of the clouds, the sun, the moon and the stars all singing praises to the God who created them. Before all this he felt very small, very insecure indeed. Again, that chill; his hair stood on end. And Adam thought, "This greatest gift, self-transcendence and freedom, this might also itself be the greatest curse!"

He saw that the sun, the moon and the stars glorified God simply in being sun, moon and stars. He saw that the mountain, the valley and the stone glorified God just in being mountain, valley or stone.

FROM THE BEGINNING

He saw that the bird glorified God just in being a bird; the tree glorified God just in being tree. And he said, "What are people? And how do people glorify God in being what God intended? How does a person in freedom, choose to glorify God? And what does that mean?" But these were puzzling matters and the creature grew tired and went down from the mountain to enjoy the pleasures of the earth. He too saw that creation was good.

So man began to build castles and empires and to accumulate great stores of goods. Forgetting about God and God's glory, he robed himself in beautiful garments and man sang praises to the glory of man. Time rolled on; birth, death, change, growth and decay. Empires were raised up and empires crumbled in the dust. God saw it all continuing under the enduring power of his creation and saw that good endured too.

But Adam grew tired of the emptiness and the nonsense of glorifying self, and in terrible frustration and anguish turned once more to God and pleaded, "How can we be persons in accordance with your purpose and to your glory? We need your vision of humanity; we need your help?"

And God responded, "The essential reality here is that I am Creator and you are creature. You'll never get anywhere if you keep on confusing those roles. You simply cannot recognize any other power, person, thing or value alongside me as 'god.' The second fundamental truth here is that you are highly valued, because I'm the one who sets the values and I say so. Therefore honor your roots, your tribe; that's who you are! The civil rights folk had it right, 'black is beautiful.' So is red and brown and everyone. Each person is fantastically precious. Therefore honor all; their property, their name, their well being, in short, their integrity as your equal, and yes that includes yourself. In short, respect the integrity of every human being including yourself. But, a caution. Watch out for that big 'I' that will continually claim center stage and try to push me aside. Its huge insatiable desire will corrupt everything you touch. Its name is covetousness. And that brings us full circle, back to my first point, confusing our two roles."

Adam took the pattern God gave him and said, "Ah, now I have

FROM THE BEGINNING

the secret of my fulfillment, my self-realization. Now at last, I can find my place in creation to his glory. But he discovered extenuating circumstances, stuff not explicitly covered, so the 'rules' had to be extended and elaborated upon. Soon it was a great system of law. Adam was so bowed down under the weight of it that he forgot that God's original plan in giving Adam the 'law' was to make him free to be, not crush him under regulations.

The centuries rolled on; birth, death, growth, decay; kingdoms arose and kingdoms crumbled in the dust. Armies, navies, merchants came on the scene and passed on. God saw the power of his Word sustaining, driving, coaxing and encouraging, And God said, "Yes."

In time Adam saw that it was not possible to rise to the glory of God through obedience to any set of rules. Even detailed knowledge of God's master-plan, his pattern for a wholesome human existence did not put the vision within reach. It was not possible for man to build the kingdom of God on earth! And the reason it was impossible was that rule number 10, against coveting. For, if man even attempted to follow the sacred pattern, he was already guilty of desiring. Never mind what is desired, it's the desiring that's the problem. It places oneself in the center of creation, and pollutes the sacred position of God according to the first rule in the pattern. In utter anguish Adam fell on his face and cried out, "We have tried, but we cannot reach you. You come to us, fulfill us that we might find our place in your power and glory."

Once again God spoke, and the thunder of his Word rolled through the heavens in a new act of creation. And God said, "This is my model of humanity." And his Word became the New Creature. We beheld his glory. Awe, wonder, perfection! It was a perfection that was a judgment on our mortal weakness. Too much; and we destroyed him. But God received back to himself, his now, Word Made Flesh.

And so it is that for centuries Christians gather and are sent to witness to the mighty acts of God in creation and redemption. They organize, form committees, make plans, set goals and exercise stewardship over an institutional church that puts flesh on his own continuing ministry. There are budgets and schedules, buildings and group studies, programs and projects. Funds are raised and disbursed. Altars are prepared, candles lighted, windows washed and washrooms scrubbed. Programs are reviewed, revised and scrapped. Sermons are preached and committees meet again and again and again. And somehow the Word has gone out ". . . all who are tired of the frustration and pointlessness of trying to glorify self. Come unto me." All who know of the impossibility of creating a Kingdom of God on earth, or of the foolishness of trying to create the Kingdom within oneself through withdrawal from the world or through obedience to a set of rules, all dust of the earth, seeking life; seek him instead and Life will find you."

And it has been heard, and people have been reached, and they have entered into the dream, the play, the joy of God's creating adventure—into his eternal life, the transcendence of his Kingdom and the ministry of his Son.

And they gather together, break bread, share in his body and blood, and sing praises to God as people were meant to do – even from the beginning.

FROM THE BEGINNING

Chaos and Creativity

Actually the polarity is chaos—order. Everywhere we look, every situation we examine includes some degree of chaos and some of order. It's never balanced, never fifty-fifty. Often there will be a lot more of one or the other. But always some mix of the two. How fortunate for us! The relative chaos offers many opportunities for our creativity.

God, for instance, started with total, absolute chaos (nothing) and so had boundless opportunity for creating. So, God created. But God didn't finish creation; if he had, there would be total, absolute order and no further opportunity for creating. What a dull creation that would be.

But God did create us "in God's image" so we could be co-creators with God—get our hands and minds into the mess and see what we could make of it. So here we are with wonderful opportunities to create and lots of satisfaction and joy in doing it. God has given us enough order to sustain and encourage us in the partnership and we have added more order—structures, principals and form—to further advance creativity.

One consequence of this is change. Nothing remains the same. And sometimes change is scary. Understandably! Some of our "creating" might not be in sync with God's idea of creativity and we err. Even then however God has us covered. In the New Creation called the

Christ, God says in effect, "Go ahead and try, and if you mess it up, I've already backed you up and you're free to try again."

So let's praise the Lord for this ingenious arrangement. If God had finished creation, there would be no further need for creative people like you and me. And if she hadn't further arranged to cover for us when we stumble, we'd be afraid to try. So let's keep chaos and change and creativity in perspective; they are wonderful characteristics of God's enterprise—and ours. And remember: Most people want progress, but nobody wants change.

EMPTY PROMISES

When I was still quite young, and being a reflective sort of kid, I stumbled upon one of those eternal truths—one of those uncompromising facts of life that grab and won't let go. And while my experience of life was not extensive, I was quickly able to see that this truth was operative for all people. People of all ages, paupers and people of wealth, everybody, regardless of circumstances had either to make their peace with this eternal reality or be destined to fight an increasingly desperate and frantic battle against it.

As I grew older, my own experience and my observations of the ways of the world broadened, and the truth of my early discovery was borne out. It is, if you will, a "law of nature," a fact of life that always holds up. That eternal truth is this: no matter how badly we may desire something—pray or work for, hope and pine for—once we get it (if we do), the meaning of it; the value of it, quickly evaporates. The promise of it turns out to be empty. Oh, we may still find the thing useful; we may even take some pride in ownership. But, at most, it will soon be taken for granted; we may even find it boring. The original promise of the desire is never fulfilled—we just come up with a new desire. It is exactly the same for the very wealthy, with their accumulation of yachts, power, vast estates, etc. as it is for the very poor in their acquisition of a new TV set.

I was a child of the Great Depression, so there were many desires never realized. But I was also a hard worker. I always had some kind of earning power and many desires were met; a new bicycle, a classy sweater to impress the girls, as an adult, a certain model car and much more. The experience was always the same. Once the goal is achieved, it's finished and another one quickly takes its place. There is no end.

Now, I'm not saying that it is wrong to want and to work for good things for ourselves and our families. The error is in attaching too much importance to the object desired. The deep yearning for meaning in life can never find fulfillment in the mere accumulation of more things.

It is as true for good fortune—that is relative to things we just stumble upon—as for those we intensely desire and work for. A survey of lottery winners has borne this out. Most winners claim that winning the lottery hasn't really changed their lives. Oh, they might live in a bigger house or drive a different car. Some enjoy more travel, and most seem pleased with the opportunity to share some of their good fortune. All this from the outside might look pretty "desirable," but the point is, from the inside—the winner's perspective—all is now taken for granted. Their lives are essentially unchanged as experienced by them.

Recently on TV news, we've seen reports of a man who won the lottery and claims he can't afford his obligatory child support payments. The smug smile caught by the photographers betrays the utter meaninglessness of his life. He was, and is, a deadbeat. Winning a pile of money hasn't changed his life one iota.

So it is that whether we desire and strive for it, or simply stumble upon it, the thing, once so full of promise, is soon emptied of its meaning.

We are speaking, of course of treasures, of things we can accumulate. All this is not true of relationships. Relationships can indeed retain value and grow over time. Paul says that love, along with faith and hope endures. Friendships can grow, deepen and last.

EMPTY PROMISES

A dent in the fender of a new car can, well, be taken for granted; those things happen. But the loss of a loved one cannot. The loss is painful, real, loaded with meaning. We can usually recover and get on with life, but we never forget. It will never be taken for granted like a once highly desired object. The relationship endures. Things can never do that. No quantity of things, no accumulation of stuff, can assure quality in life or substitute for love.

Well, in the context of those experiences and background, I read today's parables of the kingdom. How in the world can the kingdom of heaven be like a treasure found in a field or a pearl of great value?

Imagine, if you will, a peasant farmer plowing a borrowed or rented field with his team of oxen and a wooden plow in this land traversed by many ancient caravans. Travelers, frequently besieged by bandits, kept vigilant watch over their goods, and right here, years ago someone buried a treasure for safe keeping, and because of circumstances never got back to it. The farmer strikes the cask with his plow. He digs it out to see what it is, then hastily reburies it. He rushes to hock everything he has and buys that field. Now he is a rich man. What difference will it make? None. Just like the lottery winner.

Or, the wealthy merchant who, in his diligent search finally finds a pearl of outstanding beauty and value. He sells everything to buy that pearl. Now he has it, his heart's desire. What difference can it make? You know what will happen. It will sit somewhere in its hiding place and the meaning of it soon evaporates. A poor farmer or a rich merchant—it's all the same. More "things" hardly affect the quality of life. In neither case is there a suggestion that the guy in question risked anything of himself in these commercial enterprises; only his wealth is at stake. But, rich or poor the result is the same: The promise remains unfulfilled. I know that, you know it! So what did Jesus mean?

It seems to me that this is precisely the point. Jesus knew that eternal truth. He knew that many of his listeners knew. To stumble upon a treasure or finally acquire the precious pearl is ultimately of no consequence. The kingdom of heaven is not a treasure found or a pearl of great value.

But what if one did come across a treasure—a treasure so full of promise, so capable of fulfilling that eternal blessing—so full of potential as to fill one with enduring love and joy and move one to surrender everything to be part of it?

That treasure is here, says Jesus
That treasure is the kingdom of heaven.

DISTORTIONS OF FAITH

Arch rivals Newsweek and Time magazines have nearly identical covers on this week's issue—a police mug shot of O.J. Simpson. However there are two differences. Newsweek presents us with a straightforward, clear photo. Time, on the other hand, depicts a scruffy OJ, badly in need of a shave; the same photo, but "touched up" by a Time artist for (well, who knows?). The other difference is in the captions. Newsweek calls its lead story, "Trail of Blood." Time labels it, "An American Tragedy."

So it is that Time is now on the hot seat as outraged citizens and media representatives have stormed the magazine with cries of "racism." According to them, the touched-up photo makes OJ look more sinister—which it does—but additionally, according to them, it is a clear sign of racism. Well, I doubt it. They would probably have done the same with anyone's mug.

However, I too find myself offended by the Time cover, but at the caption, not the photo. The sense of it seems to be that the OJ Simpson story is the American Tragedy. Well, if he had been confined for earlier assaults this one might not have occurred. But there have been many fallen heroes, and when we look at the larger picture I certainly wouldn't call this story an "American" tragedy. There is plenty that is tragic around this old world, and much that could be labeled "national" in scope. But the "American Tragedy" in this case is the spectacle of thousands of Americans cheering OJ on, an apparent brutal murderer, as he tries to elude the police. It's that spectacle that's tragic!

We are so caught up in our hero worship—many of us—that we are incapable of getting something like this in perspective. So sympathy and support are directed to the perpetrator instead of the victim. What do we make of this tragedy in American society?

To get at this, let us consider what I call "distortions of faith." The dynamic of faith is not appreciated or considered important in our secular society. Yet it is a dimension of everyone's life, part of human "being," one of the givens. Many would deny that assertion, reserving faith for things religious. It is that denial that gives rise to the distortions. Faith is not dead in American culture; it is the culture that is only semiconscious of faith. Faith won't go away, but the people are asleep. So, faith emerges in distorted forms.

The first distortion is "religion at second hand." It's really a form of idolatry. Joe was a young man who had led an exemplary Christian life. He was a persuasive preacher, generous toward the poor and downtrodden, engaged in many good works and a standard setter for the youth of his parish. Then, overnight, he changed. He became cynical, turned in on himself and became too easily offended. Many of his friends wondered, what could have happened? Others understood. It seems that Joe's father was a member of the clergy, just an everyday, garden variety cleric, as I understood it. But Joe idolized him. Joe had him on a pedestal. Then, Joe's father stumbled. One of those stupid situations that everyday, garden-variety clerics, or any mortal, can get into. It involved another woman, and Joe's god fell from his pedestal.

This is what I mean by religion at second hand. Joe's faith was anchored in his father instead of in God. It's not fair to place one's deepest faith in any individual. It's not fair to the other, for it's a burden no mortal can bear. It's not fair to one's self; it's a set up for a sure fall. One form of this distortion of faith is hero worship. When the toppled hero is mortal, we can accept a little sin here and there; we might even, in sadness and grief, understand a terrible crime. But if the hero is god, there is no out. Our creation of idols is evidence of the deep yearning for a meaningful faith. There are other forms of religion at second hand: If I believe because the Bible says it's so, that's idolatry of the Bible. If I believe because the church teaches it, that's idolatry of the church. If I believe because the preacher, or the teacher, or the parent says it is so, that's idolatry of the person. Idolatry of book, institution or person are all distortions of true faith and no substitute for faith in the eternal God above all gods.

The second distortion of faith is clear in those situations where religion is treated as instrumental—that is, just one more power I can use to my advantage. This is the error of the so called New Age Religion. There is some appeal to it today with our big emphasis on "self-realization." But religion as instrumental gets everything backwards. It's also regressive; a reversion to the pagan religions where the attitude was one of appeasing the gods in order to advance my agenda. The Israelites didn't capture Yahweh and turn him into a leader to bring them success in their cause. That was the faith they were trying to escape. According to the Israelites Yahweh called the people, gave them a code and sent them on Yahweh's mission.

Contemporary religious fads are simply part of the self-improvement craze of the day. A discipline of daily exercise and a good diet can keep one physically fit. A routine of study and continuing education can keep one's mind keen and interests broad. All this is laudable if the purpose is to equip ourselves for ministry in the world. But if the purpose is self-aggrandizement rooted in pride, it is more fad than discipline, will likely include programs that are merely cosmetic and will set one up for viewing religion as one more resource one can use to make one a more beautiful person. Religion is not something I take hold of and use for my benefit. It is that which grabs me and calls me to surrender to it, as in "They who lose their life for my sake and the gospel's will find it." Still, all this foolishness is nevertheless evidence that the yearning for true faith is deep within us; half asleep maybe, but alive and breaking through as distortions of faith.

Finally we can consider various faith substitutes as another kind of faith distortion. The popularity of the "Star Wars" movies is one example of fairly obvious theological themes packaged for popular consumption. "The Force Be With You" doesn't presume any ultimate or final loyalty on the part of anyone. Yet such fantasies tickle our imaginations and give us a placebo so we can pretend we're practicing religion while we simply play around with it. We live in a scientific world where just about everyone knows that our "island home" is a tiny planet orbiting a fairly ordinary star among billions in our galaxy. And that galaxy is only one of billions. How insignificant we are. Yet the creator of that universe knows and loves us. How precious we are!

Yet, how dare we commit to such a belief? How dare we take our stand in such a faith? Well, there are other ways to transcend our insignificance. We can tease ourselves with thoughts of alien cultures; visitors from outer space, UFOs, beings vastly superior than us. Yes, there must be something out there; we are not alone. Devotees of Close Encounters of the Third Kind, the Star Trek TV series and so on have such zeal it must be considered a religious phenomenon. For a lot of us, these are simply good fun, good entertainment; but for others, it looks a lot more like a religion, a substitute for the real thing.

All of these are distorted forms of faith, and they are wrong! That which is phony, contrived or artificial can never fill the void left by the absence of the true and real. But they are evidence that faith is not dead; it is asleep. In dreamy half-consciousness, distorted expressions of faith arise as religion second-hand, or instrumental religion or as faith substitutes, while true faith awaits awakening.

These distortions of faith are challenges to our ministries in the world—a world hungering for true faith. The Lord of faith stirs, and through our hands Jesus comes into this sleeping world, takes it in hand and says, "TALITHA CUM." "LITTLE GIRL, GET UP." Then to us, "Give her something to eat."

ANAMNESIS

You are a teenager somewhere in Galilee. It is the year 48 C.E. A few friends, mostly adult members of your community, have gathered for some social time together in a home. You were born Jewish and have always—without really thinking about it—practiced the Jewish faith. But, as followers of the Nazarene, your family and friends are now looked down on by the teachers. They have started calling you "Christians" and won't let you meet in the synagogue any more. So, there is a beginning of the parting of the ways. You and your close friends don't really observe the Sabbath like they used to. The first day of the week has become more important. Anyway, here you are listening to the old stories.

Some of these people actually knew Jesus—personally, I mean. She certainly did, the old one sitting in the corner. She was around before anyone even heard of Jesus. She can remember hearing the Baptist preach. And she followed Jesus, along with the crowds, as he went from place to place teaching and healing. Now she just sits, legs folded under her, the whimsical, approving trace of a smile on her wrinkled face, nodding her head.

One of the men says, "Remember when he first stood in the synagogue to teach?" (Few actually remember, but they've heard the story before.) "He had them in the palm of his hand, he did. They were spellbound."

Then another picks it up. "I remember one time when there was a terrible ruckus in the street. Everyone ran out to see what it was all about. A child had fallen and scraped her knee and was crying. He stooped, picked her up and kissed away the tears to make it better." The old woman nods.

"Remember that time out in the field, a whole mob of us there were, and nothin' to eat. And somehow he comes up with lunch, enough to satisfy the whole lot."

And so it goes. You listen and watch, the ancient one nodding knowingly. Her eye catches yours. She draws you to her. You squat down to hear. "He told us to love everyone," she says, "even our enemies." "He told us many good things." With gnarled hands she clutches your tunic, draws you close; her eyes burn into your eyes and her words into your soul. "And he told us to remember him."

It's another time and place, getting on toward the end of the first century. You are an adult, a citizen of Rome. You are not exactly a well-read person, but you are aware of your country's difficulty in trying to govern such a far-flung and diverse empire. Tolerance is a principal your leaders have tried to adhere to. After all, there are so many cultures, so many religions to accommodate. There are so many gods—who cares which ones you believe in? There is, however only one Caesar, and whatever your religious persuasion, it had better not interfere with a primary loyalty to the emperor. At least that seems to be the attitude.

You do of course, know a little bit about the persistent difficulties way over in the eastern outposts of the nation with those people called the Jews. Furthermore, they have spread all over the world and they bring their strange ideas and practices with them. They just don't blend in. It's a shame, really, but no surprise that their cultural and religious center had finally to be razed. Of course, you know more about the Jews than the word spread by government propagandists. As a Christian, that's where your religious roots are. Apart from the Jewish scandal, other malicious reports have spread about the Christian sect. So there have been violent outbursts here and there. Not exactly a wide-spread persecution, but—let's face it—it's not really safe, this being a Christian.

ANAMNESIS

You go down a side street; graffiti all over the walls. Sure enough, just as you were told; there, hardly noticeable to one who doesn't know what to look for, is a crude outline of a fish. You go through a door, safe for a while with this handful of Christians. None of these folk ever knew Jesus. This is a whole new generation. There is one however, who is especially esteemed and who speaks from notes he has saved. It is said that he used to travel with Peter, so got most of his stories from one who had been with Jesus from beginning to end. His tales (this one called Marcus) sound so real and alive, it's almost like you were there. Tales of a very human Jesus, tormented in his call, with many doubts, trying desperately to come to terms with what God was requiring of him, and do it! And he speaks of a bumbling band of followers who never do catch on and who, when the chips are down, scatter like a flock of quail flushed by the hunters.

As you prepare to leave you become aware of a youth near you, another who has risked a lot to be here. You had noticed him earlier, his rapt attention while the other spoke. A word of encouragement from an elder seems called for. You take him by his shoulders. He looks into your eyes. "Son," you begin slowly and deliberately, "Don't miss these meetings unless you absolutely have to. For whatever happens to us in this crazy world, the most important thing is that we remember him."

And so it was, all over the world. In Matthew's church they remembered a Jesus who was a prophet, a kind of second Moses standing on the mountain giving the new Law. In Luke's church they remembered a gentle, caring Jesus who healed the slave's ear before going to trial. In John's church they remembered a Jesus who was God. Not a Jesus with doubts and temptations, but one who was in charge all the way, knew his script and played it through.

And so it is, that for centuries, all over the world, millions gather together regularly, often at great personal risk, to hear again the stories, to praise his holy name, to break bread together and to *remember Him.*

ANAMNESIS

PLUMB OR LEVEL

I had taken on the long overdue project of rebuilding our main bathroom. At one point—the old fixtures were gone, wires were hanging out of the ceiling, and I had torn out one wall—I was trying to resolve a structural dilemma that had confronted me. If you've ever worked on an old house you know that nothing is square. So there I was, down on one knee with a five foot level in one hand and a carpenter's square in the other, when my neighbor walked in to see how things were going. This guy is a very able handyman, so I saw the opportunity for a free consultation. "Oz," I asked, "if it is clear that you can't get both, what do you go for, plumb or level?"

"Oh, I just back off, eyeball it, and compromise," he said.

It reminded me of an incident when I was in high school during the war years and had taken a machinist apprenticeship on the side at a local factory. At one point I was in a screw machine group (a screw machine is a kind of specialized turret lathe), when I got a job order for 2,000 half-inch studs. The studs were to be made of half-inch cold rolled steel with five-eighths inch of ½-13 thread on one end. As was the practice, I didn't just accept the specs on the job order, but checked the blueprint as well. I found that the stud and specs were the same except that the blueprint called for the thread to be run back seven-eighths inch instead of five-eighths.

Now in the hierarchy of paper authority in the shop, neither of these documents outranks the other. So I went to the foreman and pointed out the discrepancy. He looked it over, then shrugged, "Oh, make it about half-way between." Well, I walked away, offended. We had the capability of working within tolerances of a thousandth of an inch, and here he was telling me that one quarter of an inch didn't matter. So, I went back to my machine and set it up to run the thread seven-eighths. I figured that if I were the mechanic putting a nut on that stud, I'd rather have a little extra thread than come up short.

These are situations where one must make a decision; the code is either unclear or impossible to follow. I remember an old banker I used to know in Idaho. He never darkened the church door, but I sort of liked the old character. He used to say, "Any damn fool can obey the law; it takes a real man to know when to break it." I liked that. So, how do we know what is wrong and what is right? The banker was distinguishing between morality and ethics. I have a fairly good sense of the difference, but just to make sure that I wouldn't mislead you, I looked them up in the dictionary. To be moral is to be "capable of distinguishing between right and wrong." An ethic is a "system of moral standards." In other words, the ethic is derived from the moral. Morality is above a particular system of ethics. And so it is that a moral person may face circumstances where to break the law is the right thing to do.

In my work as a planning consultant and trainer I try to help people distinguish between the hierarchy of purpose and the hierarchy of values that are present in any organization. The hierarchy of purpose has to do with mission, goals, objectives—that is, intended results or primary directions. The hierarchy of values governs how we will travel the way: morals. At the top of the hierarchy of values are the basics: love, justice, righteousness; the usual substance of the prophetic message. For example, from last week's readings: "He has told you, O mortal, what is good; and what does the Lord require of you but to do justice, and to love kindness, and to walk humbly with your God." We do not create values, we recognize them. They are

PLUMB OR LEVEL

over us and we stand under the values that have us!

Under the values we recognize, we adopt policies and principals. These are based on values but are formularies to guide our long-term actions and our big decisions. Still lower in the hierarchy are standards, to guide us in our day to day activities. Depending on the system, we might call these "laws" or "regulations," or spell them out as a code of ethics. There is current argument in Colorado about what the speed limit should be on the open highway. Some advocate pushing the limit up to 75 miles per hour. Others oppose the move. The value at stake here is "life" or "safety;" nobody argues about that. But how to practically and effectively spell that out in the Highway Code is up for grabs.

The Decalogue is a very high order of codification. But it too has to be "applied" to extenuating circumstances. So we have books and books of "law" and a lot of that in Scripture. But codes are always culturally biased and often based on superstition or ignorance. I can remember when women felt a compulsion to wear a hat in church. When that custom began to die out, we saw some very strange practices. Say a member of the altar guild had to go into the sanctuary and forgot to bring a hat. If nothing else was available, a Kleenex would do—but her head had to be covered.

One of the stories in Genesis that seems weird to us is the story of Cain and Abel. Why did the Lord have regard for Abel's offering but not for Cain's? It seems downright arbitrary. The story comes out of a time when the Hebrew teachers were advocating the "good" life of the nomad who kept flocks, and spurned the life of the farmer. Tilling the soil was the Canaanite life-style associated with all those pagan gods. This cultural bias comes through in that part of the story where God accepts the offering from the flock but refuses the fruit of the ground.

So, how do we know what to accept of scripture and what to be critical of? It has often been pointed out that you can prove just about anything by quoting the Bible. Chase down a story here, a tale there, and make a case for any point of view. We have just shown that God prefers cowboys over farmers.

When they asked Jesus about the "greatest law," Jesus skipped all the codes and regulations and went straight to the highest value. Love God with your whole being, and love your neighbor. St Augustine said, "Love God and do as you please." That will work as long as the first part is in place. In any case, that is the way to interpret scripture. Study it in light of the highest values; critically interpret it from the mountain tops of love, justice, righteousness. Codes, rules, regulations are so loaded with the cultural baggage of their own setting that we have to interpret them for our own time.

With that then, let us turn to today's gospel and a very harsh quote from Jesus: Do not think that I have come to abolish the law or the prophets; I have come not to abolish but to fulfill. For truly I tell you, until heaven and earth pass away, not one letter, not one stroke of a letter, will pass from the law until all is accomplished. Now that is not what I have been talking about. So, what do we make of such a hard demand to accept all the code literally—dotted "i"s and crossed "t"s?

I believe what we have here is more "Matthew" than "Jesus." This is part of the Sermon on the Mount, which is Matthew's long collection of sayings attributed to Jesus. In those days there were some Christians who claimed that the Law no longer applied to them. They were under a new covenant of Grace and could do as they pleased. That of course is a gross misinterpretation of both covenants. The ministry and witness of Jesus are continuous with the faith as set forth in Hebrew Scriptures. So here we have Matthew's Jesus taking a hard line to get those Christians back on course.

One reason I interpret the passage this way is because in nearly the next breath Jesus contradicts the sense of the quote. Some examples, still in the Sermon on the Mount: You have heard that it was said to those of ancient times, "you shall not swear falsely, but carry out the vows you have made to the Lord." But I say to you do not swear at all. "But I say to you." You see, he is interpreting. There is more. You have heard that it was said, "An eye for an eye and a tooth for a tooth." But I say to you, do not resist the evildoer. But if anyone strikes you on the right cheek, turn the other also. You have heard that it was said, "You shall love your neighbor and hate your enemy." But I say to you, "Love your enemies and pray for those who persecute you."

What Jesus is doing here is not consistent with the quote I lifted from today's gospel. But it is entirely consistent with his understanding of "the greatest commandment." He is rewriting the rules under the supreme value, LOVE.

And as moral people, that's the way we read, mark, learn and inwardly digest scripture, and that's the way we know right from wrong. Under the light of love— God is LOVE.

Priorities

We can go to a football game, dine out or see a movie. We can donate to Episcopal Relief and Development, the Red Cross or a thousand other causes. We can refurbish the living room or help paint the church . . . All worthy projects in turn. It depends on where our hearts are or, you could say:

It's a matter of priorities.

Several years ago I attended a church Urban Caucus in Louisville. There were 350 battle scarred warriors, mostly old friends or acquaintances—every color, shape and size from every walk of life—to deal with the issues: economic justice, peace, urban church renewal, undocumented people, exploitation of land and people—to press their claims as and on behalf of the poor, minorities and welfare recipients. At first the attitude was cocky, self-righteous; much talk of "them." Simplistic responses and romantic solutions were offered against complex issues. Then, gradually the hard facts, trade-offs and real options were faced. And, in humility we saw that we are all oppressors and all oppressed. So the claim and the challenge: will the church stand with the poor?

It's a question of priorities.

Back in the 1960s, construction of the Cathedral of St. John the Devine in New York City was halted. Surrounded by poverty, Bishop Donegan did not feel that he could proceed with the luxury of building a cathedral. However, in the 1970s Bishop Paul Moore and Dean Jim Morton decided to resume construction. As they saw it, this was an opportunity to provide jobs for neighborhood poor people. In the spring of 1991, Lynne and I had occasion to visit many English cathedrals. An awesome experience; how did they do it in the middle ages in the midst of poverty and disease? If we waited for the end of poverty, we'd never build a cathedral, listen to a concert, write a poem or pause to view the mountains.

Have we no priorities?

Jesus went into a man's house. The man did not greet him with a kiss, gave him no water to wash his feet. But a woman of the street came in, washed his feet with her tears, dried them with her hair and kissed them. The man asked, "Don't you know what kind of woman this is?" Jesus responded, "Where are your priorities?" The woman poured expensive ointment on his feet. Judas complained, "Hey, we could have sold that stuff and given the money to the poor." Jesus said, "Oh, I don't know . . .

It's a matter of priorities.

Many years ago women in the sweatshops got organized in a labor movement. A song came out of their efforts.

As we go marching, marching, in the beauty of the day
A million darkened kitchens, a thousand mill lofts gray
Are touched with all radiance that a sudden sun discloses,
For the people hear us singing. "Bread and roses, bread and roses."

As we go marching, marching, we battle too for men.
For they are women's children, and we mother them again.
Our lives shall not be sweated, from birth until life closes
Hearts starve as well as bodies. Give us bread, but give us roses

So much for priorities!

MAGNETIC HOME

I suppose it's natural for me to think of western Pennsylvania, northern Appalachia, as "home." It's where I was born and grew up. It is not however where I spent most of my years or the best of my years, or raised my children, nor is it my favorite turf; it's simply where I got launched. I was one of the first of my clan to kick the traces and leave. But not last; today I have family all over the country.

I grew up with a sort of romantic love of the west. So when I could, I went west: Oklahoma, Colorado in the early fifties, then the northwest; Seminary in Vancouver, then back to Idaho for ordination. I loved Idaho (much like Colorado but not so crowded) and figured it would be home from then on. Not to be! In the mid-sixties I was called to a position with our national church and moved to New Jersey. Though I lived in Jersey some 16 years, it never did feel like home. In 1971, I went into private practice, and early on had a major contract with the Diocese of Bethlehem. That's when the trouble began.

You see, I had a lot of evening meetings in the northern end of the diocese; Wilkes Barrie, Scranton, etc. Then, when the meetings were over, I'd drive south to get to a major east-west artery in order to go east to Jersey and to bed. There were two of these arteries: I-80 across the northern end of the diocese and Hwy. 22 in the south. Either would get me to Jersey and my place in central Jersey, but I usually went for Hwy 22. There were several ways south from my meetings in the north that would intersect with the east-west arteries, however no matter how I entered the clover leaf for I-80 or Hwy 22, I'd inevitably end up west-bound instead of east-bound. I knew I was doing this, so when I reached the turn-off signs, I'd carefully study them, then double check myself, and still end up heading west.

Finally one night I pulled on to the shoulder of west-bound 22 (I was supposed to be going east) and said to myself, "Now, I'm just going to have to figure out what's going on here!" So I thought and pondered and puzzled, and it finally came to me: After all those years living in the west, after driving miles and miles all over the west, I had been identifying east as "toward home" (W.PA) and west as "away from home." which, of course was accurate while I lived in the west. Now I was living and driving in the east. Oh, I knew east and west alright. It was "Toward home" and "Away from home" that were now etched in reverse on the compass of my brain. Well, figuring it out solved the problem and I had no further trouble with it.

Still, it's hard for me to believe that my roots in western Pennsylvania were so deep that wherever I happened to be, living, working, playing, raising my family, there was a magnet back there to which my compass needle unfailingly pointed. Like the homing instinct in an animal I suppose. I don't know whether it's still working.

I guess that deep inside all of us there is some sense of where one is "supposed to be," a "home!" Robert Frost said that "home is the place that when you have to go there they have to take you in." I remember a scene from a movie I saw many years ago. The movie was set in an asylum for mental patients. In this particular scene the residents were gathered in a recreation room one evening for some leisure time. Someone was at the piano, a young woman standing alongside. Then in a beautiful clear soprano voice she sang, "Going home, going home, I'm a going home." It was so touching a chill ran up my spine—I could never forget it.

MAGNETIC HOME

Then there was a time at church camp in Idaho; (we always included a few kids from the "challenged" children's State School in each camp. They were carefully selected by the school leaders and then one of their staff members would join our staff for the session. We thought this would be better for all concerned than a special camp.) On this particular occasion a group of teen age girls were sitting around on the beach; it was class time. They had gotten into a heavy consideration of the nature of heaven. Then this handicapped girl attempted to join the discussion. The kids wanted to be polite—in fact tried to be patient—but didn't really expect much; the young lady spoke, "I know . . . what heaven is," she stammered, "Heaven is . . . like . . . when you can go home, and you never - ever have to go back to the school again."

Our readings today are about home. In that dramatic selection from Joshua; the Israelites finally arrive in the Promised Land. The old slaves from Egypt have finally died off. This is a new generation now coming into their promised home, and they never, ever have to eat manna again.

Similarly, according to Paul, Christians come into their promise "in Christ" where everything has become new, everything old has passed away, and we never, ever need be at home in sin again.

Then in Jesus' parable we hear of the two good-for-nothing sons who do not know love or grace—yet, whose loving father bids both "welcome home." Let's consider that one!

On a Cursillo weekend, the official schedule calls for a first evening closing meditation by a chaplain on Jesus' parable of the prodigal son. The design for that first evening is intended to quiet things down. It's serious, somber, a real downer. Candidates would probably be inclined to go home after this talk, except there is no way out. Silence is observed following that meditation until breakfast the following morning. I've covered this assignment many times.

In my version, I don't mention Jesus' parable, I simply spin a yarn about this rancher in Wyoming who has two sons. The younger son cashes in his inheritance, buys a convertible and heads for Las Vegas. When it comes time for him to return, the father doesn't give him new sandals, robe and ring; no, a pair of alligator boots, a Pendleton shirt, a Stetson and a silver belt buckle. If it's a women's weekend, the story is about a woman who has two daughters and operates a fine restaurant. I usually get about halfway through the story before people begin to recognize it.

By the time I finish drawing out those two characters, (sons or daughters) they look so bad nobody likes either one of them. Then I scan the room and say, "Now the question for you to meditate on tonight is this: Which of these two guys are you?" Since they already know they are into a silent overnight retreat and can't discuss it with anyone, that does settle things down for the evening. I'm sure, however that my favorite line from that story is when the prodigal son, mired down in the pigsty, pauses to take stock of just who he is, "But when he came to himself," is that line. That seems to be the essential step in one's quest for home.

I mentioned my regular travel around the west. One of my frequent trips was between Idaho Falls and Boise across southern Idaho. Either way it is a long monotonous drive over sage brush covered prairie. Going west from Idaho Falls, one passes by Twin Buttes to the south, through Arco near the Lost Rivers area, then through miles of ancient lava flows, truly desolate country. It is here one comes upon Craters of the Moon National Monument; dry, deadly, fit only for rattlesnakes and jack rabbits. It is here also one will see a huge gasoline advertising sign touting the merits of the Stinker Stations, cut rate gas prices and all. These signs are all over southern Idaho. They feature a large cartoon character skunk, plus some helpful information for bored motorists. The message at Craters of the Moon is, If you lived here you'd be home now. There is no gas station at Craters of the Moon, and no conceivable reason why anyone would want to live there. If anything, one is moved to get away from this waste-land and headed for home.

But where is home? One soon discovers that the tangled clover-leafs of Pennsylvania don't lead you there; the endless interstate highways of the west don't go there. The mournful longings of the soprano tug at us, but the gas station and the open road promise nothing. In fact,

MAGNETIC HOME

we can never get there by grabbing for it. It is something that comes to us when we are open to receive it. And it is not a place on any map but a condition of the heart. Many call it "faith."

With faith there is an element of separation and an element of union. In the absence of the element of separation there is no point in faith. In the absence of the element of union there is no hope. Yet in the case of total separation or complete union, "faith" is meaningless. The element of separation appears in our experience as doubt. Thus, doubt is not a negation of faith but rather positive evidence of an enduring faith. The element of union shows up in our experience as love. Love participates with faith in expressing itself as an element of separation and an element of union. If we had total separation we would have two isolated organisms; no opportunity for love. Complete union would mean one lonely organism. 'Love' has been rendered pointless.

And so we continue our journeys in faith. There are many challenges, trials and woes, doubts and uncertainties; there are also many blessings along the way. And we stumble along and pick ourselves up again, accept a helping hand, and continue anyway.

Am I describing your experience of faith?

Is this where you are?

For if you are, then you are home now.

BIBLICALLY LITERATE

Over the years of my work as a Church Management Consultant I've spent a fair portion of that time with Canadian clients. So I have many colleagues and friends in the Anglican Church of Canada. One of the distinguishing characteristics of that church is its relationship with Canadian culture; in particular the way in which the British "establishment" church tradition has remained with it. Canadians, like Americans, enjoy freedom of religion. They have no officially recognized religion. However Great Britain, while respecting freedom of religion, does have a nationally recognized faith – The Church of England – and there are various ceremonial and public trappings that go with that. In Canada, where traditionalists still see themselves as part of the United Kingdom, a lot of that official church stuff continues in present day national life.

So it is that whenever the government has some big ceremonial something or other going on they will be inclined to find a slot for the local bishop or archdeacon. And when the Anglican Church is in charge of something big, they will try to involve local government officials in some capacity. Never mind that the local government official probably does not belong to the Anglican Church, or (probably) any church, and has precious little sense of what the church stands for anyway. But it's "traditional."

A few years ago I was doing some work in the Diocese of Kootenay (in SE BC). I appeared on the scene one day and found my colleagues all bemused as they reflected on a service they had just conducted over in Cranbrook. It was the dedication of a new facility of some sort, a community wide celebration. The church was, of course, eager to include all the proper dignitaries of the community, so the commanding officer of the local Royal Canadian Mounted Police would be a participant.

All were gathered at the appointed time in a side room before proceeding into the hall, and busily dividing up parts of the service, a familiar scene for most of us. But what should they ask the RCMP officer to do? Not too much of course. He doesn't know the Liturgy, and it's only a cameo appearance. But the Master of Ceremonies was inspired. "Here we are," he announced, "in the Prayers of the People. Why don't you do the prayer, For all captives and prisoners?"

"I will not!" he snapped back, deeply offended. It was like he was saying, "Do you know how much trouble we went through to get those guys behind bars?"

But think of the huge gap that represents. We know that we are to seek and serve Christ in all people. We know that we are to respect the dignity of every human being. We know that we forgive those who persecute us and that we pray for our enemies. We are so steeped in these basics of the faith; we don't always do it, but we believe that is what is expected of us as people of the way. But there is a huge gulf out there between us and a whole world that doesn't know any such thing.

One of the phrases we commonly hear these days is "Biblically Literate." It describes, in a relative way, the degree to which one might get away with alluding to or referencing a Biblical quote, event or story to illustrate a point—to enhance communication. In the context of a Biblically literate audience your vocabulary is greatly enhanced. If you call someone a "Judas" or a "Good Samaritan," or if you refer to a "lost sheep," or mention the "Exodus" the "transfiguration" or the "second coming" folk in that setting can follow you. When I was a kid I can recall on occasion hearing the expression "slow as Moses" and wondering about the meaning of such a comment.

But I grew up in the church and gradually came to see the point. I had become somewhat "Biblically literate." We still tend to move in circles where the population is somewhat Biblically literate. But the point I want to emphasize; there's another world on the other side of that gulf that is not. The world of that RCMP officer is a world without characters such as Moses, Abraham, Paul and Matthew, or stories such as Exodus, Noah's Ark, and a Babe in Bethlehem. In that world, Christmas has become a totally secular holiday and Easter is a springtime parade of new fashions.

Now, stop and think what it would be like to live in that world—a world in which none of these stories, characters, parables, heroes and epics is known. In casual conversation or in the daily paper, any reference to them simply passes over our heads. We have no way of knowing what they mean.

During my years of association with the Diocese of Bethlehem in eastern Pennsylvania I was quite active in the Cursillo community. That's a renewal program centered on a four-day weekend retreat. The weekend retreat is in its own right a very powerful renewal experience. The Cursillo Community has developed an extremely effective outreach program to take this renewal program into the prison community. It's called Kairos ("time"). Of course our team members selected for Kairos duty have to be especially trained in security and other matters related to prison policy and procedures. It's tough duty. My home town in central Jersey was near the Women's Prison which is where many of these programs took place. So I occasionally found myself involved with Kairos.

One of the features of a Cursillo weekend is the "Closing" on Sunday evening. Recall that the team leaders and "candidates" have been together (in isolation) for four intensive days. The whole thing has unfolded before the candidates, one step at a time with the candidates never knowing what's coming next. It has been an intense "high" for all. But now everyone is exhausted and ready to call it quits. The candidates are led resignedly into a large hall. However, unknown to the candidates, the whole Cursillo Community (not just team and candidates) has gathered to greet the new members of their Community. There is singing, cheering, "praise the Lording", "Alleluia-ing" and abrazios (hugs) all around. Talk about "support groups!" Candidates find it overwhelming.

Candidates (now "Cursillestes") are seated in a row on a raised platform facing the community. A team member makes a few remarks, then everyone cheers, waiting to hear from a candidate. The candidates, one by one as moved by the Spirit, stand and witness to their experience.

I recall one woman, mid-thirties I suppose, who had heard the Gospel for the first time and now was sure that the Lord loved her unconditionally in spite of what she had been and done. It was the story of the woman taken in adultery that had so grabbed her, a woman the Lord refused to condemn; that was a new story for her. Whoever heard of such mercy and forgiveness? And here she is, surrounded by hundreds of witnesses who are actually striving to live out that Good News; witnesses who truly believe (as she now believes) that she is a valued, holy person. Witnesses who have demonstrated that love in their love of her. She could scarcely control her emotions. She couldn't. She broke down, and wept.

Now, can you imagine what an impact it would make if we could bring that RCMP Commanding Officer into a Cursillo Weekend experience? In a way the RCMP officer and the woman prisoner came out of the same world, and given slightly different circumstances their paths could very well have crossed. But the officer had adamantly refused to pray for that woman. I dare say, the woman would have quickly agreed to pray for him.

The dilemma that leaves me with is something like this: we probably don't have much of a chance of getting the RCMP officer into a Cursillo weekend, but we did in fact have some time with him on that occasion in the Cranbrook dedication. What might we have done differently then?

BIBLICALLY LITERATE

MIRACLE ON THE SISSETON;
THE COMMITTEE THAT FAILED TO FUNCTION

It was June, still quite cool on the Sisseton Reservation in northeast South Dakota where the annual Niobrara Convocation was about to commence. This meeting is more like a very large family reunion of the tribes of the Sioux nation, mostly of the Dakotas, but today widely disbursed over the mid-west. I was present because of my ongoing involvement with the Episcopal Church in South Dakota. I had also been present two years earlier when planning had been launched for this year's meeting, the 108th, which would be the first ecumenical meeting of the convocation. Most of the church's work with Native Americans in the Dakotas bore the Episcopal label, but there had been some other missionary endeavors by Presbyterians, Roman Catholics and Methodists. There had also been recent efforts to integrate this work, thus the pending, and first, "Ecumenical Niobrara Convocation."

Two years in the planning, and now we were about to get into it. Planners had estimated an attendance of perhaps 5,000. But it's hard to know. It's all under the management of the Indians. So the usual arrangements for pre-registration, sign in upon arrival, fees per person, meal tickets, etc. were not part of the package. If you got here, you are welcome as a full voting, lodging, eating member; no questions asked. The logistics are impressive. Start with a very large open field or meadow in this rolling hill country on the reservation, mow it so people can get around, then lay it out for various functions. One might be inclined to think of a Biblical scene of Jesus on the hillside with the multitude.

Somewhere near the center of this field set up facilities for cooking huge quantities of food. A temporary post and pole structure overlaid with pine branches affords some protection from the elements. The center also includes a platform and podium for speakers and leaders. Beyond this are tables for serving the food. And beyond this, seating space for the assembly to participate in meetings. In a wide band surrounding all this is the designated area for camping, or living quarters. In a huge circle surrounding the whole set-up are the toilets. These are not molded, plastic "port-o-potties" serviced daily, but home-made wood, out-houses set over holes in the ground with the doorway facing out, away from the camp area, and some without doors. None were designated "men" or "women." A camper feeling the call of nature would take a casual stroll just beyond the camp area where one could make unobtrusive glances back to the general vicinity of the facilities hoping to spot an available unit which, when found, one quickly claimed, t-paper in hand.

Cars, campers, pick-ups and vans began arriving from the Dakotas, Nebraska and Minnesota, from as far east as Pennsylvania and as far north as Alaska. Campers selected a spot and set up their rigs; old army tents, pop-up trailers, lean-tos, whatever, were erected, staked and tied down against the fierce wind. Old friends greeted one another. Folk began milling about waiting to see what the committee had in store for them as darkness descended on the assembly.

I bundled up and went to the open air arena for a short opening ecumenical service, The Roman Catholics had this first joint service and the preacher spoke of unity in the body. Then each denominational group went to its own meeting place to line up its own business for the next few days. It was dark and cold. The wind howled. I went with the Episcopal group. We huddled in St. Mary's Church. No one seemed to be in charge. After a while one of the local clergy went forward, trying to cover for whomever was supposed to be there. It was an awkward situation for him. He tried to joke about it: "God so loved the world that he did not send a committee." But it fell flat. He admitted that they had failed to put up enough signs out on the highway to help incoming drivers, touched briefly on a couple of other points trying to buy a little time, said that he guessed that the committee had failed to function. Still, no one arrived. Then he asked, "Say, John, would you like to say a few words?"

John Two Stars was the catechist for St. Mary's; the highest ranking official in this reservation congregation. He stood up—realizing his role and the overall predicament—stepped forward and said, "Yes." He supposed he ought to say something. John was a small fellow, shy, not exactly a commanding presence, but game. He stood in front of the assembly and as he spoke he looked at the floor near his feet.

They had started planning two years ago, formed an ecumenical committee with representatives from all congregations. There were 13 Episcopal churches on this reservation; some 70 others elsewhere. The local committee met at St. Mary's. He didn't brag about successes, didn't make excuses for problems, never complained about hardships, just matter-of-factly reported their experiences.

They felt that to feed that many people they would have to raise $10,000. Everyone said that would be impossible; you couldn't raise that kind of money on the reservations. After the first year they had less than $3,000. The past year had been hard. Not only did they have to push the planning for the convocation along, they were into a major building program. A new St. Mary's would be built—L-shaped—over there to the left, a multipurpose building, larger and better than the old rundown church. Then a couple of members of the congregation died; families had to be looked after, but the planning went on.

"Sometimes," John reported, "we would have a full church for the Sunday service. We'd announce that we had prepared dinner in the Guild Hall and if everyone would come over, we could eat dinner together and do some of the work for the convocation. Then everyone would get up, get into their cars and go home. (Of course a few would come and help with the day's work.) Sometimes, I don't know how we kept going, it's working for the Lord, I guess." I was reminded of my own church, of many churches I'm familiar with, and of their struggles.

He went on to speak with some pride of how even the smallest congregations had contributed as they were able. One gave $12. His own, a fairly well established church, had donated $600. At some point the tribal council recognized the need and gave them three head of beef. Then a rancher neighbor and long time friend of the Indians gave them one beef as a memorial to his father; then another. They ended up with eight head of beef. The money dribbled in. When they finally got back to the treasurer to check, they had over $13,000.

Volunteers had been found to cart in supplies, butcher the animals, tend to the myriad of details that had to be covered. And so it was, at this opening meeting of the first ecumenical convocation, that John Two Stars gave his report of the committee that failed to function. He lifted his head, surveyed the assembly. . . "And now we're ready," he said quietly, "We can feed 5,000!"

PILGRIMAGE

I lift up my eyes to the hills—
From where will my help come?
My help comes from the Lord,
who made heaven and earth.
He will not let your foot be moved;
he who keeps you will not slumber.
He who keeps Israel will neither slumber nor sleep.
The Lord is your keeper;
the Lord is your shade at your right hand.
The sun shall not strike you by day,
nor the moon by night.
The Lord will keep you from all evil;
he will keep your life.
The Lord will keep your going out and your coming in
from this time on and forevermore.
(A Song of Pilgrims)

Everybody is supposed to make a pilgrimage to the temple in
Jerusalem at least once in a lifetime. Not alone of course, more like

a guided tour. It's a time of rejoicing and celebrating—and a time of high risk and fear. But it is traditional; a tradition everyone should honor. The ancient ones tried to keep the tradition alive even in the times of the first temple. They would gather in groups in far-flung corners of the realm and come parading, marching and singing into Jerusalem. We are marching in the light of God. Dancing, banners waving, balloons swaying, but the hardships and the dangers are real too. No rest stops, no port-a-potties, no clean sheets or room service. Bands of thieves roam the hills looking for an unguarded moment to raid the camp and raise havoc with the travelers.

So we have formed our own little band to travel to the Promised Land. We might not all make it. But others will discover and join us as we travel. The little ones skip and run down the dusty trail scarcely aware of the dangers. We trudge along, heavily burdened by what seems to us to be the necessities of life and travel. Along the way, as we are able, we maintain the ritual observances; and we look after one another, with extra attention to the very young, the elderly, those with special needs, and for those hurting today in body or spirit. We pitch our tents in the evening. Get the youngsters bedded down.

Now it is dusk. We are worn and weary from the day's trek. So we mingle, more than a little apprehensive, around the camp fire. We have posted sentries on the hillsides around the camp. But will we be able to sleep? A raid could come at any time. The bandits have certainly been watching us all day from their hiding places in the hills just beyond the camp. What if one or more of our sentries dozes off? They're all just as tired as the rest of us. Listen to the voices as various members of our company observe, and wonder:

I lift up my eyes to the hills. Yes, the sentries all seem to be in place and alert—for now! But can we count on them? Can the vestry really get us through all this? Does the rector know what we're up against? Do we have what it takes to see it through? Well, where is our help to come from? A cold chill runs down our spines, a shiver. We sense another presence in the hills all around. Our help comes from the Lord; Yes! Yes, the Lord, not from those stupid little bronze castings of some of our neighbors, which, when trouble comes you have to scramble to save them. Not from the power of positive thinking, nor our own doggedness. No, the Lord who made heaven and earth. The Creator of the whole cosmos, that's who! The Lord.

More voices: He will not let our feet slip. He will not let our faith grow faint nor our courage wane in the wilderness. Unlike our sentries—it's getting darker but we can still make them out, and they are still on duty—unlike the sentries, or the rector or the wardens, who might nod or doze, be distracted and miss something. And unlike the bishop (It's not his issue, we brought ourselves here, it wasn't his idea.) Yet, the one who does watch will neither slumber nor sleep. It is the Lord God himself who is our keeper. The God of Abraham and Sarah, of Isaac and Rebecca, of Jacob and Rachael; the God and Father of our Lord Jesus Christ—our God, who watches; who keeps vigil.

What about shelter? Not just from thieves and bandits, but from the elements. Sunstroke and dehydration threaten too. We need shade from the sun. But the Lord is our shade at our right hand. And water? Yes the miracle of water; the water of the chaos out of which God created in the beginning; the waters of the Red Sea and of the Jordan parted by God to open a path to the Promised Land; the water of baptism in which we are buried, and raised in Christ. And so we feel blessed—with protection from our enemies, with shade, with water— on our trek in the wilderness. And with protection from the evil spirits. So the sun will not strike us by day, nor the moon by night. Yes, according to some of the elders evil spirits are associated with the sun; sunstrokes are intentional, the purposeful action of an evil force. Same with the moon, only those devilish spirits practice their mischief under cover of darkness and their target is the mind. Lunacy it's called, the source of it being lunar or moon demons. So, we seek protection from the sun by day and the moon by night, all the time alert to the probability of raiders' attempts to attack us.

There are many sorrows, dangers and woes on our pilgrimage, many pitfalls, many temptations. But it is the Lord who keeps us from all evil, who keeps our life! Who watches over our going out and our coming in. The Lord is our real sentry; not our own swift hand,

PILGRIMAGE

not our own quick foot, not our keen intelligence, not our 'loyal' buddies nor our 'true' allies. And not even those kin-folk over there on the hillside standing watch, diligent as they are; it's the Lord we count on, from this time on and forevermore.

So, we've been on this trek a full year now, and as with those on any pilgrimage there have been trials and tribulations as well as rewards, joys and satisfactions. We have certainly experienced our share of both. But the journey continues and we continue in the faith that "the Lord watches over our going out and our coming in from this time on and forevermore." And we are ever mindful of the vision, the dream and the purpose which led us into this venture in the first place, this venture we have come to refer to as our trek through the wilderness to the Promised Land, our "Jerusalem" so to speak. Our pilgrimage now takes us into the season of Advent, then through Christmas, Epiphany, Lent, with a vision of

> New resources to work with,
> New challenges to delight us,
> New pilgrimages calling us
> New life in Christ blessing us,
> on into Easter and the Promised Land.

THE PATRIOT

I see in the news that there's a big renewed controversy over the pledge to the flag. It seemed that the Sunday closest to July fourth would be a good time to pick up on that. Of course, the controversial phrase is, "under God." Those words were not always part of the pledge, and they were probably inserted for the wrong reason. But I support keeping them there and I support retaining our national motto, "In God We Trust."

It's not that I support imposing some or any religion on anyone. I also support the principal of the separation of church and state, and our constitutional mandate against the establishment of any religion. I firmly believe that religion is healthier and stronger where the government stays out of it.

While I'm at it, let me also say that I'm opposed to officially sponsored prayer in our public schools. That would be way too subject to abuse and impossible to monitor. I'm also against any law that would forbid burning or "desecration" of the flag. "Desecration" means to defile something holy or sacred as in a church or synagogue or mosque. The flag is a symbol of our nation but it is not sacred; to treat it as a sacred object brings us right back to the establishment of religion, "Americanism." It would pain and distress and thoroughly

THE PATRIOT

disgust me to see someone wipe their feet on the flag. And I would feel that they are stupid, insensitive, ignorant and repulsive. But I'd still have to stand on the side of protecting their freedom; otherwise, who are we?

Now all these are matters upon which honest people might disagree. So, I'm not asking you to accept my point of view. But I do ask that, as people of faith, with me as your spiritual guide, you consider my point of view. There is a common thread running through all this that I'll pick up on in a minute. But first I wanted to let you know where I'm coming from so we can get that one out of the way.

I speak to you as a genuinely patriotic American. One who can get emotional and teary eyed watching the flag waving in the breeze—not one of those huge things over a used car lot; that's obscene; But one on a proper pole at a government or military installation, or someone's home. I speak to you as one who might experience a chill run up my back at a good rendering of our national anthem. The best I've heard in a long time was a Canadian baritone at a special tribute following 9-11. It was a straight-forward, quality performance that made the hairs of your head stand up. Too many American soloists seem compelled to add their own little trills and yodels that I find much more distracting than enhancing.

I volunteered for service in the USN Seabees at age 17 near the end of the Second World war, and I know what it feels like to stare down the barrel of an enemy cannon. I supported Truman's decision to drop the bomb. (Another matter on which honorable people may disagree.) But there is a reasonable possibility that it saved my life. My buddies and I were being prepared for the invasion of Japan, no question about that. An invasion would have cost thousands of American and Japanese lives. Then the bomb! My unit was diverted to Okinawa where we spent the balance of our time building roads and airstrips. Furthermore my two brothers and all my male cousins; 15 – 20 I suppose, served in that and subsequent wars of our generation. Between us, we had every branch of the military and probably every theatre of war covered. Incidentally, I wish someone

THE PATRIOT

would teach our president how to properly salute. That little jerk he does is embarrassing. Anyway I speak out of some experience.

So, back to that laundry list of issues and positions and the common thread running through them. It has to do with how we understand true patriotism. True patriotism is not idolatry of our nation. "My country right or wrong" is not acceptable; it's irresponsible! True patriotism recognizes that we are a nation under judgment, always under judgment. John Gardner of Common Cause fame, writing of the turmoil of the sixties said "It's like we are polarized. On the one hand we have the unloving critics: "down with the system – tear it apart – start over again!' And on the other, the noncritical lovers with the "my country right or wrong" attitude. "Don't touch anything!"

What we need says Gardner, are loving critics." And that comes close to my definition of true patriotism. A true patriot is one who truly loves his or her country and who works diligently to correct her faults and clean up her blemishes. The patriot is not one who denies or tries to hide the problems.

So, when I say, "one nation under God" in the pledge, it is a reminder to me that the nation itself is not an idol; it is not our highest point of reference. It is, bottom line, under judgment. Now I wouldn't argue for the precise term "God." To me the operative term here is "under." We could say "one nation under the highest values that we as a people share." That would work for me and maybe it would work for the atheist. Kind of wordy; "God" abbreviates it. The real point in all this is that the nation is not god and must never be permitted to behave as though it were. I am certainly not out to define "God" here or elsewhere in our national papers or on our currency. We can discuss what "god" means to us as theologians or as Christian community; but as Americans we do not try to impose our sense of it on anyone else.

It is not an inconsistency, in my opinion, that we provide for religious services for our armed forces and accept public prayer on public occasions such as in Congress, but do not permit prayer in public schools. Religion is an important part of who we are. A member of our military is not obligated to participate in religious observances. Chaplains are screened not only by their own denomination but also by the military, so are well prepared to serve without prejudice or imposition. They are there for people of every, or no faith.

As for other public occasions, sponsors are always under the scrutiny of the press as well as the public and we are free to ignore or participate as moved by conscience. We should, however, allow some latitude as these are sensitive areas. In the case of schools, we are dealing with children who are impressionable and with teachers who wield an enormous amount of authority over their subjects. Besides, who will decide which prayer? Will it come out of The Book of Common Prayer or the Koran? Will it be according to Baptist tradition or Buddhist? It's way too messy; better to stay out of it.

Now, having said all that, I must also admit that, for most Americans these are probably not matters of grave immediate concern. They pop up now and then, get some airing, then quiet down again. It is not that they are unimportant by nature. It is rather that our founders largely resolved them generations before our time. Praise God for their insight and courage. Our liberties are a precious gift. But it is up to us in every generation to understand, affirm and preserve them. So considered, our greatest enemy today could be our own complacency.

Laity (La'i ti)

I looked it up in the dictionary. Ah ha! Just as I thought. Webster has it wrong. No wonder it is so difficult to clean up this word. "The people as distinguished from the clergy," or "those not of a certain profession, as law, medicine, etc. as distinguished from those belonging to it." A lay person, according to the dictionary, is a person who is not, as distinguished from a person who is. Why, that's discriminatory. Besides, the world already has us in enough trouble pointing the finger at people who are not or who are less or who are different." We can do better than that.

Laity (laos) means "the people of God," or, all baptized people—all Christians. It's an inclusive term. So when you use the word "laity" please don't leave me out just because I'm ordained. I want in; after all I am baptized. Ordination doesn't set one apart in some exclusive class. It recognizes one for particular ministries, but all the baptized are authorized for ministry.

"Ministry" (I didn't bother to look that one up) is sharing God's gifts with one another. We each have a unique assortment of gifts or talents. Collectively, we have an enormous array for cooperating with one another in the interest of getting things done. Most people in the world have "jobs," "trades" or "professions." The payoff for one in a job is a salary; nothing wrong with that as far as it goes. But Christians—that is, mechanics, homemakers, teachers, priests, plumbers, nurses, etc.—have "ministries."

The payoff in this case is the sense of being called and sent, of, "this is where I'm supposed to be." The difference is in the heart not in the duties one is responsible for. Indeed, the duties might be identical but for one it is a "job" and for another, a "ministry." One might experience it as enslaving drudgery and another as blessed privilege. One might feel entrapped, another freed. One of the clues to discovering one's ministry is paying attention to one's gifts. Another is heeding the call when it comes. A third, or maybe the first is, don't fall for that crazy notion "But I'm only a layperson."

HIDE AND SEEK

You remember playing hide and seek as a child! It starts quite young: "peek-a-boo" with tots, then progresses to a child's game with a "home base" hiding and tagging those found. Part of the game is not hiding too well; it's no fun if someone is not "found." Watch kids in this sport; if too well hidden, they give themselves away. Not being found is no fun.

Then we grow up and it's no longer a child's game but the game of life. And it's serious business, so we hide; behind make-up, behind titles, behind status or "success," behind clothing, including vestments, the latest fad or hair-do, behind the roles we create; mother, father, scholar, priest, teacher, nurse. . .

But in this serious business there is some risk that we might indeed hide too well and not be found. The masks behind which we hide are to some extent also intended to reveal, so we live in the tension – to hide too well and not be found, or to show ourselves. For to not be found is to be lost; alone. In this serious game of hide and seek we hope that some way, someone will truly discover who we are and that we will truly come to be known. So we seek for some way to "give ourselves away."

This place of being found and known—of finding and knowing the other—this place is called relationship. And the state of being in this place called relationship is known as personhood. What the game of hide and seek is really all about is becoming persons. And this becoming persons is absolutely and without qualification the first and most important agenda in human development. It is more important than health, job, food; more important than living or dying. It transcends all of these and endures beyond them. By comparison, all these "necessities" of life can be seen as simply means, the real point of life being to become person.

It is not a simple challenge and we can't ever claim to have finished the job. But we can do it to some extent. Hiding is the easier part. It's the "giving ourselves away" part that is the more difficult. But it is only in giving ourselves to another that we find ourselves as persons in relationship. There is a real possibility that we might go through life seeing others as mere objects, things; and if everyone else is a thing, then I too am a thing; merely one object among others; an it rather than a who.

There's risk involved in getting into a relationship with another person. The act itself requires a certain amount of trust or faith. We have to believe that the other is, at least somewhat, open to the possibility of the relationship. One has to be vulnerable. One must count on the vulnerability of the other. If the guards are all up there's not much chance of reaching the 'person' behind all that armor. So it is really a matter of mutual trust and mutual vulnerability and maybe of some initial testing before jumping head first into the mystery.

I well remember a senior high camp one summer in Idaho. I was the dean of this camp several years running, so had a chance to assemble a highly qualified staff of volunteers. This particular year we had a young lady from one of our churches who was new to the camp program and unknown by our staff. Campers were assigned to "cabin groups" of six or seven per cabin for sleeping quarters. Each member of our staff was also assigned to a cabin as "cabin counselor." One of our counselors, Wanda was one of our best; mature, secure, as loving as they come.

We had been given some advance warning about the young lady in question from her rector. She was in Wanda's cabin. From our regular staff meetings we soon began to learn a little about the girl nobody knew. She was armor-plated. She was also deceitful and untruthful and nobody, so it seemed, could reach her. She had her guard up so high nobody could touch her. Wanda, at one point exclaimed, "I've got my neck stretched out this - - - far! She could whack it off any time, but I don't know what else to do." Nor did anyone else. So the program moved on through the week. All in all, a good camp, but one youngster, so it seemed, completely out of it.

At this same camp we had a young man, Clarence; late twenties probably, from the state school for the handicapped. Clarence had been with us for several years and more or less knew the ropes. He loved to ring the big bell on the stand outside the mess hall. Clarence had virtually no verbal skills. However, he was quite imaginative in his use of "uhs" and body language, and with a little patience you could usually get the drift what he wanted to say. This severe limitation didn't discourage him the slightest. He'd keep trying as long as his listener was willing to stay with it. He did seem to comprehend what others were saying.

Since a lot of our programming was decentralized, we used the period right after lunch (when we were all together) for announcement time. As dean, I'd chair this very informal period. I'd stand, wait for things to quiet down, then ask if anyone had anything they wanted to say. Anyone could stand and have the floor for a few minutes. On the final day of camp, lunch was our final session together. Then the bus arrived, picked up the campers and departed for its big loop through the towns and villages of southern Idaho, delivering campers to their home churches throughout the diocese.

Needless to say, boarding the bus for home and all the prep, clean-up and packing getting ready for departure was an extremely emotional time for all involved. New friendships had been forged, promises made, new identities tested; and of course, reunions could be expected—they are all part of the same diocesan church. Many of the strong leaders of the diocese gained their initial sense of diocesan

HIDE AND SEEK

identity through experiences at church camp.

Anyway we are now at our final lunch for this year's camp experience. As I said, it was a good camp. There were some pastoral concerns, but that's to be expected. Now, for the last time for this camp, announcements! I stood and waited for things to quiet down. Campers were a bit impatient with last minute details on their minds before boarding the bus. The first hand to go up was Clarence's. You could almost hear the sigh, but courtesy ruled as campers patiently waited to decipher whatever it was that Clarence had to offer.

Clarence groaned and uhmed and motioned—then finally walked around the dining room to the girl we had all been so concerned about. His sign language continued to no avail until another young lady camper got it. She translated for the rest of us.

It seems our problem girl had been approached by Clarence for help in writing a letter. (We encouraged kids to write home while at camp.) She had patiently listened to his grunts and groans and eventually gotten some kind of message together that satisfied Clarence, and addressed and posted the letter. We never did figure out who the letter was sent to or what it was about. All Clarence wanted to do now was to publically thank the girl for helping him; an entirely appropriate gesture for the occasion. The young lady broke down sobbing. Many witnesses wept with her.

So it was one year at Senior High Church Camp that a bumbling staff conducted an ordinary camp program through which the Lord led a very marginalized, severely handicapped young man to reach out to a girl in need of relationship. And led this troubled young lady with all guards up to respond to the "safest" human being at hand, risk vulnerability, and achieve one grand step in her journey toward personhood. Then all the campers got on the bus and departed unaware of this story of God's Grace. But then I don't know the other stories, do I?

THE LITTLEST ANGELS

The question is often raised, why did the angels bring tidings of great joy to the shepherds? Luke makes it sound, well, sort of romantic. But, think of it, those guys were out there in the field for weeks on end. Campfires, no change of underwear, smelly, dirty, wheeeew! Why wasn't the revelation delivered to Caesar Augustus, or Governor Quirinius, or the high priest and the scribes, or to the Pharisees, or Sadducees? Why not let the important people know what was coming down? Even Joseph and Mary had to get the news second-hand. At least, that's the way it seems from Luke's account.

Well, as I've said before, there are large gaps in Luke's report. However, I do have access to other, non-canonical sources and I can explain what actually happened. When the time drew near for the baby Jesus to be born, the Lord called the angel Gabriel in for orders. "Gabe," the Lord explained, "My Word is going to come to my people in a way unheard of in history—an INCARNATION—a way never to be required again. Now I want you to get that message out to all people in every corner of the cosmos and through all time from the beginning to the end. I know I can count on you to get that done."

So Gabriel called a Planning Council meeting; a command performance for all angels, archangels and the whole company of heaven. Together they plotted the strategy. They had maps and addresses of the whole universe and their schedule covered all eternity. One of the entries in that huge blueprint (I saw it!) was this parish. Assignments were parceled out to all present and every heavenly messenger knew exactly what part he or she was called to do.

Well, almost all. There were two little angels there who had never been on a mission before, Allie and Ralphie. While the maps were being studied, they had their copies upside down. And when they went over the zip codes, Allie and Ralphie nearly always read theirs backwards – as in Hebrew – instead of left to right. When it came to dates, they had been told that neither the American nor the Canadian system of short hand notation had been blessed in heaven, so they were never sure whether the day or the month came first. It was quite obvious that they were set up for some kind of grand foul up. However, not one of the heavenly host noticed this and Gabriel adjourned the meeting thinking that all was ready for his "go" signal.

Meantime on Earth, Mary and Joseph were making their way toward Bethlehem. On this particular day it was getting quite late and cold, and they simply had to find a place to lay-over for the night. Then Joseph spotted a fire on the side of a hill and knew right away that it must be a sheepherder's camp. And indeed it was. The shepherds quickly gave them something to eat and then found them a good place to bed down for the night. They were soon fast asleep as the shepherds watched over their flocks and their guests.

No sooner did they get to sleep, but they were awakened by a strange eerie sound like a screech, and they opened their eyes to behold two silly looking little angels; halos askew, harp chords all tangled up, trying to sing something or other. It was a discordant and miserable performance. Mary rubbed her eyes and laughed; "What in the world are you two up to?"

The shepherds stood around in a circle, dumb-founded. Ralphie spoke up, "Alleluia! Behold, we bring you great tidings of good joy . . . er, good tidings of . . . Allie, how does that line go?"

THE LITTLEST ANGELS

110

Mary said, "Oh I see what this is about, but you are too early, and in the wrong place." Allie looked at her wrist watch, then at Ralphie. "She's right, it's only half past 4th Advent. People won't be ready yet; can't be expected to be. It wouldn't be fair to spring this on them with no warning whatsoever. Well, what can we do now?"

Joseph tried to be reassuring; "Hey, no harm done, just consider this a dress rehearsal, and we'll see you again in a few days." Next morning, after some goat milk, curds, dates and bread, the couple continued on their way. The shepherds also left; time to lead their flock to fresh pasture.

Sometime later we find the angels, archangels and the whole company of heaven anxiously pacing around on red alert. The two littlest angels were with them too. With some experience behind them, they now had their act together and could sing with the best of them. Then Gabriel's signal came, and swish! They were out of there in an instant, immediately infiltrating the whole cosmos and all of history all at once. Impossible, you say? With God and quantum mechanics nothing is impossible—taking the message that God so loves the world that he gives his only son.

Now there is one thing about revelation that I should remind you of; and we've been reminded of this all through Advent. Revelation comes only to those who are open, or you might say, ready— expectant—prepared! Nobody else gets the message. Nobody else hears the angels. They don't experience the awe, see the lights or feel the thrill. So, you see there's the answer to the question: Why the revelation came to the shepherds.

On that holy, blessed night, with all God's angels singing "Alleluias," and "Glory to God," and, "To you a Son is born" throughout all creation, there was only one small group of shepherds on a grassy hillside near Bethlehem who were open and who heard. And it just might be the case that the reason they were ready was because of two over-zealous little angels who got the time and place wrong and alerted the shepherds, and Mary and Joseph, in advance!

So it is that every year about this time, God's angels are zipping all through creation, getting the Good News out once more to all those

THE LITTLEST ANGELS

111

open to it—that God so loves the world that he'll pay any price.

And you're probably wondering, how do I know all this? Well, you'll remember I mentioned seeing that long list of appointments? Well it was Allie and Ralphie who showed it to me. And the reason they showed it to me, I think, was that opposite the posting of our church for this year were the assignments, "Allie and Ralphie." I guess they just wanted me to know.

Anyway, I just wanted you to know, that if I got all this right, Allie and Ralphie and Associates are scheduled to sing here tonight! Of course only those who are ready and open will experience it. For others, nothing; no thrill, no bright lights, no heavenly music—nothing. It's only for those who are ready!

Choir bursts in: (several bars of the Alleluia Chorus)

THE LITTLEST ANGELS

SINGING A NEW SONG

The Russian Empire has crumbled; the persecuted people of the states that once comprised that oppressive system search for order and identity; for peace, for hope and prosperity.

In South Africa apartheid has been dealt a death blow, and the people struggle to bring about justice and reparations for thousands, and to create a form of democracy that can work.

Here at home one financial or commercial enterprise after another has failed and even General Motors stumbles and gropes like a severely wounded giant.

All over the world—chaos, confusion, greed and conspiracy are wreaking havoc. Yet stronger powers prevail and will prevail: faith, hope, grace, and love. And all over the world people find the will and the courage to sing to the Lord a new song.

And what are we to make of that?

In the 8th century before Christ, the Jews in the Holy Land were living in a divided kingdom. Judah in the south centered on Jerusalem, and Israel in the north centered on Samaria. So it had been for over 100 years, since the breakup of the Davidic kingdom after the death of Solomon. King Uzziah reigned in Judah during much of this century. His reign was characterized by order and prosperity. As such things go, these were good times for Judah, and Uzziah was a good and loved king. However, toward the end of his reign, Assyria, to the east and north was building its military might, extending its borders and becoming a threat to the whole region. For the two little Jewish kingdoms it must have felt something like Kuwait with a Saddam Hussein breathing down their backs. After over 40 years of stability and prosperity under King Uzziah, and now with serious threats on the horizon, the beloved king died. It was 742 BC. And now, with the loss of their king, very unsettling times for Judah.

That same year a young priest was in the temple tending to his duties when he was struck by a vision and called to a ministry of prophecy. Isaiah reports the event in detail in the sixth chapter of the book that bears his name. "In the year that King Uzziah died, I saw the Lord sitting on a throne, high and lofty, and the hem of his robe filled the temple." It is a dramatic scene and ends with the words, "Here am I, send me," and the beginning of a long ministry.

Some 10 years later we find both kingdoms in disarray. Idol worship is rampant, corruption prevails, and the Assyrian threat has become even more imminent. Samaria, the northern kingdom, is squirming and compromising all over the place to avoid the impending doom, and Ahaz, a thoroughly corrupt person himself, takes the reins in Judah. It wasn't terribly hard to read the signs of the times. Two small Jewish nations that had bargained away their souls, and a giant just over the hill, ready to gobble them up.

Chapter Seven reports on Isaiah's attempt to reach Ahaz and get some sense into him. This is the chapter where we find another of the prophecies commonly read at Christmas: "A sign will be given to you; a young woman will conceive and bear a son and call his name Immanuel." Now get the sense of this. He didn't say that the child would be "God with us." But that giving birth to a child and calling him Immanuel would be a sign. God is with his people through all kinds of trials and tribulations. But stupid Ahaz doesn't know it or doesn't care. The prophecy is a word of encouragement for anyone who can hear. God is with us. Immanuel.

SINGING A NEW SONG

But Ahaz does not heed. So Isaiah attempts to take the message to the people. This is reported in Chapter Eight. But they don't listen either. So Isaiah, with a remnant of believers, goes off to await another day. During the interlude, about 723 BC, the northern kingdom is sacked and the people disbursed throughout the Assyrian empire—and that's the end of Samaria as a Jewish land, and of the 10 tribes that comprised it.

A few years later, 715 BC, Ahaz dies and the young Hezikiah takes the throne. And with this, there is renewed hope that true worship will be restored and righteousness prevail. And, it is generally thought, this is the occasion for Isaiah to come out of seclusion and sing to the Lord a new song—our first reading this evening from the ninth chapter of Isaiah:

The people who walked in darkness have seen a great light
Those who lived in a land of deep darkness -
on them light has shined
For the yoke of their burden - and the bar across their shoulder;
the rod of their oppressor, you have broken.
For to us a child is born - to us a son is given
Authority rests upon his shoulders, and he is named
Wonderful Counselor, Mighty God Everlasting Father, Prince
of Peace.

Again the prophet gives a word of encouragement. A new opportunity is given to us. Here is a king with whom we can work. "To us a child is born, to us a son is given" A new king in the lineage of David. He is not foretelling an event still 700 years away. He is interpreting the signs of his time and giving the word of hope. So why bother saving the manuscript? How was it important to generations to come? Because there is a transcendent, timeless quality to the utterances of a great prophet; every generation needs the reassurance and confidence—perhaps a sign—that God is with us; we have not been abandoned. So for hundreds of years Hebrew scholars studied and pondered prophecies such as these. And for them—in persecution, in captivity, even through the Holocaust—they have found in these passages the promise of a messiah.

The early Christians, of course, saw those promises totally and eternally fulfilled in the coming of Jesus the Christ. And for Christians of all times the Christ is not just the sign, but also the eternal reality of God with us. Yet Christ died for all people, not just those who know how to call upon his name. And so it is that this night—in Asia, Europe, Africa, the Americas—all over the world where people suffer from hunger, deprivation, persecution, injustice, people – even those who know not Jesus of Nazareth – somehow sense the reality of God with us. That grace, love and hope will prevail, and like Isaiah and the psalmist, they sing to the Lord a new song. But for Christians this night the words are:

To us a child is born.
To us a son is given.

Job's Kids

Job's sons used to take turns hosting parties in their homes, always inviting their three sisters to join them in their merry-making. When the parties were over, Job would get up early in the morning and sacrifice a burnt offering for each of his children, thinking, "Maybe one of them sinned by defying God inwardly." Job made a habit of this sacrificial atonement just in case they'd sinned.

It's called a contingency plan. It wasn't that Job doubted the integrity or the word of his kids. But what if one of them overlooked something? You can never tell; kids get so caught up in what they are doing, so busy, so preoccupied with the business at hand even if the business is having fun. They can get absent-minded, even careless. So, better to play it safe. It certainly won't hurt to offer a little sacrificial atonement just in case someone got a little too exuberant in their celebrating or a bit reckless in their game. Yes, better to play it safe.

Now, as I say Job did trust those youngsters. He knew they would always choose the good, the true, the beautiful over the ugly, the false and the evil, *if it were in their power to choose.* But what if someone else were calling the shots? What if they were the victims of someone else's horseplay? Or what if there wasn't any perpetrator? Crazy things do happen even when no one's at fault, and yet there still may be victims. Job's kids were good kids. Nobody ever said anything to the contrary. But kids will be kids. They can get to assuming that they're invincible or immortal.

Job just wasn't taking any chances. He couldn't protect them from every hazard on the freeway, steer them clear of every pothole or shield them from every stupid driver. He couldn't repair every injury or fix all the dents, and he certainly couldn't heal all the raw nerves, broken hearts, bruised egos and crushed hopes that were predictably going to arrive on some unpredictable schedule. But Job could trust in the Lord and pray for the best.

And that's where the sacrificial offerings came in. So Job faithfully and regularly laid his offering on the altar all the time praying fervently that the Lord receive and understand the immeasurable value of all that was at stake in this simple action. Given the circumstances what's an old man to do?

THE CHOSEN

Hi, I'm Gabriel—You know, messenger of the Most High—with a message. I've been on the job a long time, and I'm here to tell you, when you've been on the job as long as I have you get to know the Chief fairly well. Now I want you to know that I'm a very faithful messenger. I always follow orders to the tee. However that doesn't mean that I always agree with them. No, we do have our disagreements, and sometimes I make a point or two. But when He gets that look in his eye and says, *"It's my choice!"* I know the arguing is over, and it's time for me to get to work.

I can remember, for example, when you all got started. The earth was a beautiful place back then. Well, you know, it's still beautiful, but then it was so . . .innocent. What with the wind, showers, lightening, the great oceans and continents, forests and grasslands and flowers, and all those animals—all blissfully ignorant—of the wonder of creation, of the awe of a creator, just there. Not a question or a rebellious thought in their simple little brains.

Then one day I could see that something was going on in His head. He called me over. I didn't know what to expect. "Gabe," he began, "My creation is truly a work of art, and you know how I love it, every bit of it from a tiny grain of sand to a majestic mountain, from the smallest buttercup to the great whales. But there is nothing out there that knows I've been creating, nothing that knows about my love for it all, or is capable of loving me. I'm going to put a new creature in there, something that is, well, a little bit like me; a creature that can know me."

Of course I could see the implications right away and the argument was under way. "Oh no, Lord," I protested, "You can't do that. Your creation is just fine as it is. Why spoil it? If you put a critter like that in there, it'll have self-consciousness. It'll run rampant in its freedom. It'll have a sense of morality, knowing good and evil, and you can bet that it'll choose evil at least half the time. Why, a creature like that will think that *it's* God. It'll never get that part straight."

But he squared off, looked me in the eye and said, *"It's my choice!"*

So, that was it! He made you a lot like the other creatures. Yes, true creatures you would be, but somehow with a spark of God in you. And he showered you with blessings and put you in a beautiful garden with just about everything you could want. But, of course I was right. Within just a few days you traded the whole park for one bite out of some nondescript fruit and you were out in the wild scratching for a living.

Well, the centuries rolled on, much as I predicted. There was idolatry, murder, even wars and slavery. Kingdoms and Empires flourished and were ground down. Some lorded over others and there were even some who believed *they* were God. Now God's love was still there too, so there was joy and blessing as well. But it was no Garden of Eden and it just didn't seem to be going anywhere.

Then one day the Lord called me in again, for another assignment. "Gabe" he announced, "I'm going to adopt one of those tribes, make it into a holy people, a priestly nation which will then be my instrument for blessing all the people."

"Well, Chief," I responded, "That sounds like a good idea." Then, trying to be helpful you know, "You could adopt the Egyptians, they're great builders. Or, better yet, why not choose the Greeks; great philosophers and thinkers . . . or, (my mind raced ahead) you could

THE CHOSEN

120

wait a few years for the Romans to get in place (Time doesn't mean all that much to us, you know – forward, backward, sideways – it's all the same.) Romans are good organizers. Or you could wait a few more years for the Americans to get their act together, then you'd have the advantage of all that wonderful technology."

"No, Gabe," he said, "I've already picked out the ones for this job. It's Abraham and Sarah over in Ur. But I have to get them away from the influence of their own people so they can get off to a new start. So you get down there and lead them off somewhere to the west."

"But Chief," I came back, "That's just about the dumbest idea you've ever come up with. Why, Sarah's barren, and Abraham is a dried up old fig tree. Those two old geezers haven't had an original idea cross their minds in 80 years. How can you make a nation out of them?"

I should have known. *"Gabe, they're my choice!"*

So I led them out of Ur into the land of Canaan. They did eventually have a son, and the tribe flourished. So the idea of a called people at least got a start.

However, it was just a matter of a few generations and the whole bunch of them found themselves enslaved and persecuted in Egypt. I figured if the Chief was going to do anything about his plan for a priestly nation, it was about time to bet on a different horse—pick on a nation that showed some promise, you know. But the next time he called me in it was to inform me that he had chosen Moses to lead his people out of Egypt. "Moses is over in Midian right now," he said, "I want you to go down there, call to him out of a burning bush and give him my orders."

"But Moses is a murderer," I protested. "He's a wanted man over in Egypt, you send him there and they'll hang him!"

But you know how it goes: *"He's my choice!"*

So it is with the Chief. He's always redeeming and calling into service the most unlikely people. He made a hero out of Rahab, a professional prostitute. Jacob was a cunning thief, stealing from his and his wife's families. David was an adulterer. Ruth, a foreigner, used her sexual prowess to make it into the Davidic line.

THE CHOSEN

So I guess I shouldn't have been surprised when he called me in to go over his most outrageous plan of all time – to personally come into his own creation as a real human creature and to save it from the inside. I'll have to admit that sounded exciting, and my mind immediately raced ahead to a vision of this extraordinary event. I saw a tall, handsome, strong, David-kind of figure, dressed in ermine and purple, with a gem-studded crown, prancing into Jerusalem on a high stepping Arabian stallion—what a figure. I was just thinking you know, didn't say anything.

He went on with *His* plan. He would arrive as a vulnerable, helpless infant, same as every other human. And he would do this through a couple of inexperienced, unmarried, peasant teenagers. I had all kinds of arguments; too risky, impractical, unbelievable, but, as usual: *"They're my choice!"* And, as usual, I would be the messenger.

Well, after pondering it some, I thought, hey, that won't be so bad. To have the privilege and pleasure of going down to that cattle shed. I could pick up the little baby, cradle him in my arms, kiss him – my own Lord! Then explain it all to Mary and Joseph. . . no, wrong again. My orders were to take the whole heavenly host, in rare singing form, and offer the revelation—in the middle of the night, mind you—to a band of smelly, ignorant sheep herders encamped on the side of a hill miles from anywhere. *They* would explain it to Mary and Joseph.

Now, if there is any consistency in the drama of the Chief's dealing with his people, it has to be in this irony. He always insists in calling into service the least promising, the most unlikely characters around. It's a consistency that stood up during his brief years on your planet. Look at his chosen associates; uneducated fishermen, conniving tax collectors; and women (would you believe) a loose-living, foreign woman at the well, another caught in adultery, and so it goes.

Well, as I say, I'm only the messenger – and now you've heard the message! I'll try to sum it up because you're not supposed to forget it. First, while the Chief loves all his creation, he has a passion for the downtrodden, the poor, the meek, the sick and those hurting. There is no sinner beyond his redeeming power, no mourner beyond his comforting peace, no life that is unimportant. The second part, if you can hear it, is really the same. "Tell them," He said, *"You are my choice!"*

PRAYERS ANSWERED

When I was, well I suppose, about five years old, I had the earliest experience of prayer that I can clearly recall today. You see, I had a puppy—more like a half grown dog—and my puppy was sick.

In those days of the Great Depression most dogs didn't have pedigrees and few ever saw professional health care. So, under my father's guidance, I was doing what I could for my sick puppy and that included a lot of praying; at least every evening at bedtime. However, things progressed to the point where the pup was in considerable misery, and I remember praying one night, oh so desperately, that the suffering would end—meaning, of course that healing would come.

When I awoke next morning the dog was dead. So it was that a big mystery overtook me for the next few days, of exactly how God hears and responds to one's desperate prayers. "Wow," I thought, "This is powerful stuff. One has to be careful about what one asks for."

My puppy was no longer suffering and I distinctly remembered, that is exactly what I had prayed for, an end to suffering. But that wasn't what I had had in mind. God had misunderstood me and granted my prayer literally. It wasn't God's fault; it was mine. I hadn't made my prayer clear enough. As I pondered these things, I came out of the experience convinced that prayer is truly powerful, but one has to be quite careful about how one formulates the prayer, or risk being misunderstood.

Well, I suppose that was okay for a five year old. But the point I want to make of it tonight is that God really does hear our prayers; our petitions, our praise, our thanksgivings, and God responds. However, in our finite wisdom we may not understand the meaning or see the relevance of that response. To us, it may seem that there is no response at all. God's response might be so much richer, fuller, bigger than anything we can imagine, that we miss it all together.

The great prophet Isaiah preached in the last half of the eighth century BC. There were other prophets of this period: Amos, Hosea, Micah. And there was plenty to preach about. The period saw, to mention one incident, the fall of the northern kingdom to the Assyrians and the disbursal of the northern 10 tribes. Now, to get things into some kind of time frame, let's remember that in about one thousand BC, David had unified the nation and expanded her borders, and he and his son Solomon had ruled for some 80 years. These were years of glory for the Israelites. However, upon Solomon's death the kingdom fell apart. Then we saw a northern and a southern kingdom, and kings came and went, until, in Isaiah's own words, "In the year that King Uzziah died," Isaiah, in a vision in the temple, received his call—some 180 years after the death of Solomon.

During this time, and, in fact, for hundreds of years after, the Jewish people diligently and sometimes desperately, prayed for a new king, a king in the line of David, a king who would rule in justice, with compassion and righteousness. They yearned, they sacrificed, they prayed, and above all perhaps, they tried to obey Torah in order to be worthy of such a king. In fact, some claimed that if only everybody would obey Torah perfectly for only one day, Messiah would come and usher in the perfect kingdom. "Messiah" meant "anointed one." That is, a human being completely ordained to God's service.

Well, the nation had a lot of good kings over the years, anointed to God to serve God's people. And they also had some bad ones. But none of the good kings were perfect, and the realm of God did not come. Trouble from outside the borders and sin within the community persisted, and the people paid. But the prayers and the sacrifices of the people continued, and their hope would not die.

It is in this context that we read the oracles of Isaiah. Or, more particularly, the one we just heard read. It is a word of assurance to the people that their prayers have been, or will be answered. Scholars can't quite make out whether Isaiah speaks of some king or prince about to take the throne, or whether he points to better times in the future. But it is clear that he speaks of an earthly king in David's line. In their theology the idea that their transcendent God—creator of the universe—could become king in human form was simply unthinkable. Listen once more: *For a child has been born for us, a son given to us.* ("Child" here doesn't mean "infant" it means "child of God" as you and I are children of God.) *And he is named Wonderful Counselor, Mighty God, Everlasting Father, Prince of Peace.* (These sound like divine labels, but they are examples of oriental exaggeration. Put them in the context of the culture and we can hear them as intended. For example, imagine an Arab today in the presence of a king, "Greetings, O holy one, may you live forever.") *There shall be endless peace for the throne of David and his kingdom. He will establish and uphold it with justice and with righteousness from this time onward and for evermore.*

So, Isaiah says, "yes, yes" this will be fulfilled. There were many other such prophecies: that the king would be born in Bethlehem, that he would be a suffering servant atoning for the sins of the people. So the yearning and the prayers and the hope continued through the centuries—for the messiah, the anointed one of God to usher in a new age. It continues today.

The story is told, out of World War II and the persecution of the Jews, that at one point, a mass grave was bulldozed out, people were lined up and machine gunned, then abandoned. There, in the bottom of the hole, a few survivors found each other and took stock.

Among them was a woman in labor. In due course she delivered a boy. One old man who had assisted her, wrapped the babe in rags, cradled him in his arms and said, "Who but the Messiah could be born in a grave?" The baby lingered for a few days, then died. But one has to admire the depth of the faith of a pious old man who lived in the tradition of the prophets and even from the grave found reason for hope.

Let us now shift to another scenario, some 700 years after the time of Isaiah. And let us respect Luke's sense of the ironic. Luke provides the setting: when Augustus was emperor of Rome and Quirinius the local governor. And let us conjure up a picture in our mind's eye of the grandeur of Rome at that time. See, in the image of a Hollywood production, the military might and order, the chariots, the banners. The empire extended from the British Isles in the west, well into the Orient in the east. We worry about our infrastructure. Rome had it, grand and extensive; highways everywhere, signs at intersections so travelers could find their way. A somewhat arbitrary and fierce justice, but order was maintained. Then, over in one far-flung corner, the Jewish religious establishment with its High Priest and scribes, Pharisees, Sadducees, money changers in the temple . . . take in the picture. This is a very busy, urban and important setting with lots of VIPs. Keep that picture in the back of your mind as we continue with Luke.

Against this background of important people and activities, an angel of the Lord appears to a handful of dirty, smelly, ignorant peasants at night as they watch over their sheep, and says, "Come on over to a certain stable in Bethlehem. The Lord is about to give you a sign."

And so begins the Good News of Jesus the Christ, the Son of God, the Messiah. To be called a revelation, it has to have two sides. On the one hand, we must have a bearer of the revelation—Jesus, in this case; on the other, just as important, the receiver. Now for most of the people praying for a king who would be the perfect anointed of God, ushering in an age of justice and peace forevermore, it was beyond human comprehending that in response to their prayers, God himself

PRAYERS ANSWERED

127

would come into the world, fulfilling all the prophecies, plant the seeds for a new age, and bring the peace that transcends the foibles of history—the peace that passes understanding. But a few did receive him. As John puts it, "To all who received him, who believed in his name, he gave power to become children of God, who were born, not of blood or of the will of the flesh or of the will of man, but of God. And the Word became flesh and lived among us."

And so from that time, two great religious traditions have flourished; sometimes tentatively, side by side down through the centuries. We stand firmly in one of them. But tonight as we praise God for sending his son into the world for the redemption of the world, let us also, in humility and gratitude, praise him for the nearly 4,000 years of life and witness of our sisters and brothers of the Jewish tradition who live on in hope and continue to make powerful contributions to our own theological heritage.

Apathy, Anyone?

We were seated in pairs—facing each other, knees together. It was part of a workshop on chancel drama sponsored by the young people of the parish. The instructor explained the exercise: the idea was to see what could be communicated through touch alone. While one partner in each couple kept her or his eyes closed, the instructor wrote a word on the chalkboard then erased it. The other partner then proceeded to poke, pat, stroke or hug the other in a manner intended to communicate the sense of the word. Then with everyone's eyes open, the instructor asked the "blind" partners how they interpreted the attempted communication. Sometimes the meaning was conveyed quite well; care, comfort, grace. After checking, the leader again wrote the word on the board, now for all to see.

It was my turn to communicate. My partner closed his eyes and waited expectantly. He could hear the chalk hitting the board and I watched as the letters of the new word—APATHY—appeared and were then erased. The expression on my partner's face turned to anticipation and readiness. I just sat there—couldn't think of any way to express that one. He waited hopefully. Without moving a muscle, I stole sideways glances at other pairs. They were all trying. But, I thought, no matter what I do he will misinterpret it. So I just sat there helplessly and looked at him. He was straining blindly to pick up the most subtle movement or signal. "Maybe I missed something," he seemed to be thinking. But I didn't move.

Finally time was called and all eyes opened. My partner looked at me, mystified, disappointed. I avoided his eyes. The leader started on the far side of the room. "What did you experience?"

"Uh, anger?" "Disgust?" No one was sure. It was a guessing game. He turned our way. "What did you feel?" My partner gave me a brief glance seeking some final clue, but got none. Hesitantly, he turned toward the instructor, "Nothing!"

APATHY, ANYONE?

SAMUEL AND MARTIN

Some things just don't seem to change that much over time. Our first reading for today takes us way back maybe 3,000 years, before the consolidation of the separate tribes of Israel into one viable nation, before Jerusalem was made the center of public worship and the temple was even dreamed of, certainly before the glorious reigns of David and Solomon, actually even before there were the kinds of reliable records we would be inclined to call "history."

In those days stories were passed from one generation to the next orally, by pure memory. However, the ancients seem to have been very good at that. Some exaggeration here and there probably, but all in all the record appears to be quite credible. Stories passed on in this manner prior to writing them down are referred to as "Tribal Memories." One of the tests of the reliability of such records is the extent to which the account, as received by us, appears to "whitewash" the story. This certainly does not seem to be the case in the stories we have today. The warts and blemishes all show even in the heroes.

Our story today is the call of Samuel in the midst of a thoroughly corrupt religion. Religion was not just corrupt, but largely ignored by most of the people. Eli, a devout man in spite of the sorry state of things in his time, was maintaining a modicum of observance at the shrine at Shiloh. And Eli's two sons (priests at Shiloh) were as corrupt as any of the crowd, scraping the cream off the top of the offerings of the people, laying with the women attendants at the shrine, and Eli, unable to stop any of this!

However, there was a certain devout man in the region, Elkanah who had two wives. One he dearly loved, Hannah who was barren. The second, Penninah, was prolific. (In that culture, a woman was assumed to be fertile and expected to be productive.) Elkanah, with his family, made an annual pilgrimage to Shiloh to "worship and sacrifice." These were distressful times for Hannah who was reminded of her inability to have children and, at the same time, a big opportunity for the smug Penninah to flout her string of offspring. On this one occasion, Hannah prayed fervently that the Lord open her womb and give her a child. In fact, she promised that if she had a son, she would dedicate his whole life to the Lord. The Lord heard her prayer and Hannah conceived and bore Samuel. She kept her promise, and after the child was weaned (say about three years) she again went to Shiloh, this time to present her son, dedicated to the service of the Lord, to Eli. Today's reading sums up the meaning of Samuel's witness in the opening, middle and closing verses. By this time Samuel is a lad of about 12 years of age. Hear again those verses:

The word of the Lord was rare in those days; visions were not widespread. This is not a description of a silent Lord, of an absentee Lord, of a Lord on vacation. In fact it's not a description of the Lord at all. It's descriptive of deaf, uncaring, indifferent, numb people. A people incapable of hearing the word of the Lord, blind to the visions of what might be, what should be. This is the world the child Samuel was born into. This is the world the saintly Hannah was willing to give up her child for, with no sense of how it all might play through.

Then we come to the call of Samuel. But how is Samuel to understand what is going on? Now Samuel did not yet know the Lord, and the word of the Lord had not yet been revealed to him. So Samuel didn't know what to make of a voice coming to him in the middle of the night. Samuel! Samuel! But wise old Eli saw that something was going on with the child and could provide council. He told Samuel to go lie down again and wait, and if he heard the voice again answer, Speak Lord, your servant is listening. This Samuel did and he did indeed receive the word of the Lord that night, and finally there was someone in the land open to hearing the word of the Lord.

Finally, in today's summary of Samuel's ministry we are told, *as Samuel grew up, the Lord was with him and let none of his words fall to the ground. And all Israel from Dan to Beersheba knew that Samuel was a trustworthy prophet of the Lord. It's like saying, "All America from Boston to Los Angeles knew that the word of the Lord was in their midst!"*

So, Samuel is born into a world in which the word of the Lord was practically unknown and there were no visionaries to provide guidance to the people. But as Samuel matures and gains credibility, that world becomes one in which the voice of the prophet reverberates throughout the land "from Dan to Beersheba." What an awakening that represents. What a transition! And that story would continue to unfold until a thousand years later a child would be born in the line of David who would be hailed *MESSIAH—God with us*—and we have been celebrating that date for 2,000 years. It all started when a devout woman prayed fervently to God and vowed to offer her son in service to God. (Not totally unlike the vow of another woman many years later who said, *Behold, I am the handmaid of the Lord; let it be to me according to your word.*) And Samuel came into the picture to complete that transformation begun through a woman at prayer.

This weekend we observe the life and witness of Dr. Martin Luther King, Jr. The Word of the Lord has been heard by many prophets over the intervening years; Amos, Hosea, Isaiah to mention a few of the ancients, many more over later times and a respectable number in our own day. One of the most significant of those events, falling in the tradition of Hannah and Samuel was surly the moment the Word of the Lord called out *Martin! Martin!* And the unhesitating response was *Speak Lord, for your servant is listening!* I can't tell you exactly when that happened in the life of Martin Luther King,

SAMUEL AND MARTIN

but it obviously happened somewhere along the way, and from there the young pastor went forth, not only in the tradition of the prophets, but also in the tradition of Gandhi and other non-violent advocates, to suffer plenty of violence before police dogs, fire hoses and brutal police officers. His *I have a Dream* sermon, goes down in history, along with Lincoln's *Gettysburg Address* as one of the classics of American political oratory. And his unswerving dedication to nonviolent tactics in spite of the violence that inevitably came his way is a profound witness to the Prince of Peace who initially called out his name.

It was Saul Alinski, famed community organizer, pacifist and student of American democracy, who pointed out that in a situation where the opposition has all the guns, the strategy must be one of "moral Jujitsu." The point being that if the other side has all the real power, our side will have to swing public support in our favor and win over the opposition in the eyes of a sympathetic public by maintaining the moral high ground. This was all a Gandhi or a Martin Luther King could do. Thus, the strategy is to very carefully select the battle ground knowing that the enemy can be counted on to use stupid and violent tactics, and thus give us the day in terms of moral jujitsu. This is, of course very risky. People can and do get hurt. Both King and Gandhi were eventually assassinated. Yet even this is part of the price in such confrontations. This is serious business and great prophets are willing to take the risk and pay the price.

So today we celebrate the vision and witness of the prophet. Dr. Martin Luther King, Jr., Samuel and many others who see conditions others scarcely notice. Conditions are after all, only "conditions." One might say "mere conditions," normal, acceptable, usual conditions, part of the tolerable state of things we have grown comfortable with, some bad ones, to be sure, across this land, but there are always problems.

It is the call of the prophet to see ISSUES where others see mere conditions. Issues are conditions demanding attention. It is the call of the prophet to turn mere conditions into Issues. It's the prophet who jams issues into our faces until we do see them and have to take action. So let us praise the Lord for the life and witness of Dr Martin Luther King, Jr., and the whole historic prophetic tradition starting at least with Samuel who was one of the first who heard the call and responded , *"Speak Lord, your servant is listening."*

THE QUESTION OF PURPOSE

*On the evening of Wednesday, October 27, 1993 there was a
devastating car accident a couple of blocks from the church involving two
young women on their way to church. A near term infant was lost, and
both women seriously injured. The congregation responded admirably
in looking after the families, but by the end of the week, many were
emotionally drained. Then on Sunday we gathered for Word
and Eucharist.*

WHY?

That's the question that's always asked whenever there is a tragedy.

WHY?

An earthquake in California or India.

A hurricane in Florida or a flood in Iowa.

A fire in Boulder or a conflagration in Laguna Beach.

Or a car accident in Thornton—and somebody dies.

WHY? WHY?

But it's the wrong question!

The question "Why?" implies purpose. Since there is no apparent
human purpose and the question won't go away, it turns to God.

What was God up to? What is God's purpose in this tragedy?

Then we struggle to find answers to the wrong question.

"Because God is punishing someone—me!"

and the crushing burden of guilt.

"Because God called him home. He's in a better place now."

Pure escapism; an attempt to shield ourselves from the terrible weight of the truly tragic.

But all the answers are wrong because the question was the wrong question. And the only answer to the question "Why?" is, "There was no purpose." There was no human purpose. There was no divine purpose. There was no human or divine intention at all. It was not a part of any plan on earth or in heaven.

The event was utterly devoid of purpose. Tragedy is purposeless, and that's part of what gives tragedy its devastating power. When someone dies in battle they die for a purpose, a cause. But when someone asks of a tragic event, "Why?" the only answer is a ruthless, uncompromising, "There was no intent! There was no purpose in heaven or on earth. No design, no plan. It was aimless."

We are creatures of creation, and vulnerable; vulnerable to natural disasters. Vulnerable to the foolish errors of one another, and things can happen. The tragic event is, almost by definition, without purpose!

BUT NOT WITHOUT MEANING!

Purposelessness is not the same as meaninglessness. Yes, "purpose" and "meaning" are frequently used interchangeably as though they meant the same thing, but they do not.

Purpose has to do with intentions, goals, plans. Meaning has to do with values, relationships, ultimate reality. Purpose has to do with building a new Denver airport. Meaning has to do with what we do with a new airport once we have it; and even how we go about building in the first place. Putting purpose in is a characteristic of human enterprise and identifying the purpose precedes the event. Getting meaning out of it is of the nature of God's enterprise. It follows the event; it comes in retrospect. A tragedy is utterly void of preceding purpose, but it is never lacking in proceeding meaning.

This is the redeeming work of God, and God can work with anything we can throw at her.

Furthermore we all know this.

Tragedy strikes; it's devastating. In its aftermath we stand dazed, uncomprehending, overwhelmed; facing the chaos, the emptiness of our own lives. Alone, hopes and visions shattered, plans, purposes, dreams, intentions—all dead. But over time, God's redeeming grace comes powerfully into play. New perspectives are discovered. Lives are changed; new depths, richer meanings, new life—resurrection. The tragedy is still a tragedy for any feeling person, still painful, still without purpose, still remembered. But now, in God's work of redemption, it is loaded with meaning.

We have all witnessed this, perhaps in our own experience. Someone is put down hard, totally crushed by some senseless event. And sometimes they don't recover. But usually, over time and with God's grace, we see new life shinning forth. A deeper, richer, more fully human being is redeemed from the ashes of tragedy. A miracle of God's healing grace.

There is another common response to tragedy, not just the question, "Why?" but the complaint, "It's just not fair." That's right! Tragedy is not fair. It strikes at random, and anybody might be in the way. It's not fair.

But then neither are Grace or Blessings fair! It seems that there is some tragedy and some grace along the way on everyone's journey. And then it seems there is a lot more of one or the other on some journeys. And that's not fair either. But let's not treat these two, tragedy and grace, as having equal weight and as though some fate or god should apportion them out fairly so that everyone gets a balanced share.

There is a qualitative difference between tragedy and grace. Tragedy is of this world; it is of creatures and existence and creation. It strikes, raises havoc, causes pain. But it is transient and redeemable. Grace is of God; it is eternal and, like the peace of God, it is beyond understanding. It transcends worldly events. And grace has the final say!

Paul, in mulling over these matters, put it this way:

No, in all these things we are more than conquerors through him who loved us. For I am sure that neither death nor life, nor angels, nor principalities, nor things present, nor things to come, nor powers, nor height, nor depth, nor anything else in all creation, will be able to separate us from the love of God in Christ Jesus our Lord.

Amen

EASTER TIMES FOUR

With four versions of the Gospel at hand we are inclined to mentally merge them all into one homogenized translation. Yet, they are much more interesting in their distinctions. Take the Easter story for example: Mark is the oldest Gospel, written about 70 AD or thereabouts. Here is his account—or her account; nobody knows who wrote any of the gospels.

Very early on the first day of the week, three women approached the tomb; nervous, apprehensive, puzzling over how they would get that huge stone blocking the entrance rolled away. Not to worry. Someone had already done it. They went into the tomb, but the only thing they saw was this young fellow in a white robe sitting over there on the right. He tried to explain things to them, but all he managed to do was scare the living daylights out of them. They took off like scared jack rabbits and refused to discuss it with anyone.

End of story. Mark just leaves it there—a mystery. It's good story telling; kind of leaves people thinking. However, there is always someone in the crowd who feels compelled to "explain" stories to others to make sure they get the point. So it is that sometime later someone else added another dozen verses.

Matthew may have been the next gospel to be written. His account gets pretty dramatic:

It was getting on toward dawn. Two women were approaching the sepulcher when the lightening crashed, the earth shook, the guards fainted and this angel zinged in from the sky, rolled the stone out of the way (showing that the tomb was empty) and then sat—right there on the stone. Well, that just about did the women in. They didn't know whether to shout "Hallelujah! Praise Jesus" or scream out in panic. Anyway, this angel, all decked out in white, explained the situation and then sent the gals out to go tell the guys that Jesus would meet them all over in Galilee. They were just getting started when Jesus stepped out of the bushes and said, "Hi there." That was almost too much. But Jesus reassured them and sent them on their way.

Meantime the guards came to their senses and realized they were in hot water—the empty tomb and all, nobody would believe them. So they made up a story about how the followers of Jesus had robbed the grave. Sometime later Jesus did meet the disciples on a mountain over by Galilee and gave them the Great Commission. End of story according to Matthew.

Luke was written about the same time as Matthew or perhaps a little later. If Matthew was dramatic, Luke was poetic. His account was so popular his friends talked him into doing a sequel: the Book of Acts. Luke's Easter story is kind of long, so I'll condense it here.

It was early dawn, first day of the week, when the women, who had gathered up their ointment and spices for tending to the body, came to the tomb and found the stone already rolled away and Jesus missing. They just stood there wondering what to make of it, when two men in dazzling apparel appeared from out of nowhere. The women shook in their sandals. But the messengers prompted, "Don't you remember what he said?" Then—click—they got it and ran off to tell the guys who didn't believe them anyway. "It was just woman talk!"

However, sometime later two of the men were out for a walk when Jesus joined them and explained the facts of death and life. They high-tailed it back to Jerusalem to share the good news with the others. But while they were explaining it, Jesus again appeared and asked, "Hey, you guys have anything to eat around here?" They did. After his snack Jesus hung around for a little teaching. (His disciples could hear things now that they had never understood before.) Then he told them to stick around town for a while. He promised to come back, and upon his return he'd really juice them up with the power they'd need for the job he would be assigning them. Then he blessed them and left. End of Luke's Story!

However, Luke takes it up again in The Book of Acts. Early on in that book Jesus does return. It's the story of Pentecost followed by the earliest accounts we have of the start-up of the new church.

John's Easter story includes an account of Pentecost, but one much simpler than Luke's. This Gospel was written sometime around the end of the first century.

It was still dark on the first day of the week when Mary Magdalene got to the tomb and saw that the stone had been removed. Well, that was strange! Suspecting that someone had stolen the body, she ran off to tell the others. Two of them ran back to the tomb, found the linen cloths, but nothing else. Could it be…? They went home.

However Mary hung around crying her heart out. When she chanced to look into the tomb she saw two angels in white. They wanted to comfort her, but then the gardener caught her attention and she thought he might know something. However when he spoke her name she saw that it was Jesus. What joy! "I have seen the Lord," she told the others.

That evening the disciples were hiding out in a locked room when Jesus somehow walked in and said, "Shalom." Then he blew on them and said, "That's the Holy Spirit; you are now empowered for ministry."

Now Thomas was out of town when all this was going on, and when they told him about it, he just refused to believe any of it. So, eight days later while Thomas was with the group Jesus returned and Thomas was convinced. But, Jesus said, "So, you had to have your proof! Well, from *now on nobody gets any proof; but those who believe on faith will be richly blessed by me."*

End! Actually, John adds a brief postscript to underline that point about faith. Sometime later another writer added another whole chapter to John's book—more resurrection appearances. But it's easy to see that the original book ended as I've shown.

So, that's it; four reports of the resurrection. If we could arrange for four modern day reporters to cover the event we'd also have four personal accounts; each one reporting from a distinct background, for a particular client group, interested in specific details and putting their own personal spin on things. The four accounts we do have were written over a time period of several decades. All things considered, I think we have a reasonable report on what the early Christians experienced.

If, on the other hand some ancient spin doctor or editor had gone over these reports in an attempt to maintain consistency and assure that we would have no reason to doubt any part of it, these reports would surly look quite different today, don't you think? We don't need to worry about how many angels were at the tomb, or just who rolled that stone out of the way. The important point is that a bunch of very ordinary folk who had fumbled and bumbled along after Jesus, never quite understanding what he was up to, suddenly become charged up, empowered to get out there in the world and launch a church. Now the story of Pentecost is certainly an important part of that whole report. We'll be picking up on that in a few weeks. Today, we have the Easter stories: An empty tomb overflowing with life for everyone. That's a full plate for now I'd say. We'll get back to the rest of the story.

EASTER TIMES FOUR

Hands

Signs of spring—melting snow, returning robins, splashes of tulips, trees in blossom and blisters—all get mixed up here in Colorado. A late snow falls on new green leaves while the robin scratches to find materials for a nest. But the blisters are a clear signal that the season has, in fact changed. The tender hands into which I've been pressing the bread all winter suddenly are presented—still tender—but with blisters. They appear on the inside joints of fingers, most typically in the V between thumb and forefinger. Then I know; they've been out raking, spading, hoeing. It's spring!

There are other hands at the communion rail presenting other messages the priest is privy to. The rancher in Idaho presents hands with thick fingers, callused from a lifetime of handling ropes, fencing tools, and from pitching bales of hay. The millworker in Pennsylvania presents a different pair of hands; thick heavy fingers, yes, but callused mainly on the finger tips from handling hot steel or sharp bolt threads spun on a lathe.

Then there are the dainty, almost feminine fingers of the surgeon. He hasn't known the heavy, knuckle-breaking work of farmer or machinists, but his hands are likewise mechanically skilled in the delicate work of scalpel and suture. Or the red hands of the mother of three; changing diapers, bathing, feeding, laundering. What a challenge to hands.

There are the chubby, eager hands of the tot who knows that she is part of, whatever this is that is going on. And the gnarled, arthritic hands of age; hands that can sign and hands that direct; hands with rings, scars, missing fingers. Open hands, crossed hands, prayerful hands. Here every Sunday of the year and one hardly notices. But now it's spring, the blisters appear and the priest is moved to see and ponder—hands. Two thousand years of hands; blessing, healing, nailed to the cross, reaching out to receive the bread of life.

A ministry of hands serving the World, now offered to receive their Lord, blisters, scars and all. Ministries of tending the ill, feeding the nation, providing our material needs. And my hands, which have done many of those things too, take the Bread of Heaven and press it into these hands. Then we go in peace to love and serve the Lord—all these hands.

COMING TO BELIEVE

The Word we have just heard was the first part of the twentieth chapter of John's Gospel. He closes his account with these words:

Now Jesus did many other signs in the presence of his disciples which are not written in this book. But these are written so that you may come to believe that Jesus is the Messiah, the Son of God, and that through believing you may have life in his name.

John wrote this Gospel for his church, his congregation. His church was made up of converted Jews and some Samaritans. They lived, studied and worshipped somewhere in Palestine, and they were a couple of generations removed from the events we have been reliving these past few days. John writes so that this small community of believers might grow in their faith and have life in his name.

So, let's consider this question: how is it (according to John, at least) that we might expect to come to faith and grow in faith? Well there are some peculiar characteristics of John's Gospel that set it apart from the others and that make clear what we should not expect as a means of coming to faith.

For example, we should not expect some miracle. In another part of this chapter John tells us of Thomas' experience. Thomas, you recall was the one who said that he would not believe unless he saw the risen Christ with his own eyes and actually felt his wounds. Sometime later, Jesus did appear and Thomas saw, and touched the wounds, and cried out "My Lord and my God." But Jesus said, "So you had to have your proof—from now on nobody gets any proof—but blessed are those who believe on faith." Now we do hear of occasional miracles, but John's clear message to his flock is: Don't expect a miracle to bring you to faith.

They just installed a new bishop over in Western Massachusetts. Reporters interviewed his 11-year-old son on the occasion who said, "It's really a great job and you can really get close to God." Well, we can smile at a child's enthusiasm. But I can tell you this. John would have no truck with status. We live with popes and archbishops, bishops and cardinals and priests. We wade through the protocol of "The Rt. Rev," "The Most Rev," "The Very Rev;" whether to use Mister. Father, Doctor. John would have ignored all those formalities. We are all brothers and sisters in Christ. Oh, he knew about all that stuff. It was there in his day too. But he chose to ignore rank and titles and status.

Paul also had to contend with such rubbish with the church in Corinth. Oh yes, he said, we have apostles and prophets and teachers and healers (He always mentioned apostles first—he claimed to be one.), but all are equal, he tried to persuade them. We face the same issues today. Go to a big service at the cathedral sometime and you'll see that each rank and position has its own peculiar vestments and other symbols of office and proper place in the procession. Then we, like Paul, say, "But, of course everyone is equal."

John had a simpler way. He just ignored all status terms. An apostle is one who is called and sent. Most bishops today think of themselves as modern day apostles. A disciple is a follower. So all apostles are disciples but not all disciples are apostles. In the other three Gospels those closest to Jesus are apostles. Other followers are disciples. John never uses the term apostle. All followers are disciples. John

COMING TO BELIEVE

never hints at rank or status. You don't get "really close to God" by becoming a bishop. John's brothers and sisters could grow in the faith, but not through rank or promotion.

Being male in a male-dominated society provided no advantage in coming into the faith either, in John's world. The first coming to the faith for anyone in all four Gospels is evident in the utterance: "You are the Christ, the son of the living God." That evidence of dawning faith is attributed to Peter in the other three Gospels, but to Martha, according to John. Neither did ethnicity count; Luke tells us of the early, post resurrection preaching of the apostles—when they converted thousands. John doesn't mention that but does tell us of the Samaritan woman who, in the name of Jesus, converted a whole village while Jesus was still alive.

For John coming into the faith has nothing to do with miracles, status, sex or ethnicity. So, how does it happen? Well according to John, growing in faith has its roots in being a part of the community of love. The whole Gospel is full of this message. The First Letter of John has been called the greatest hymn to love ever written. You'll recognize these quotable phrases: God is Love. Love one another as I have loved you. No one has greater love than to lay down his life for one's friends. How does God's love abide in anyone who has the world's goods and sees a brother or sister in need and yet refuses to help? Little children, let us love, not in word or speech, but in truth and action. We love because he first loved us.

And on, and on, and on!

Love is the Ultimate Reality in which we live and move and have our being. We are the people of Love—of God; for God is Love. Love is the pattern of relationships which define community—a community nourished in the sacrament of Christ's life, in Word, expressed in care for one another; a community in which all disciples are affirmed without regard to any kind of status. This is where and how coming to faith and growing in faith happens—in Christian Community.

Now, let's see how this works out for the three saints in today's lesson; the figures at the empty tomb, how did they come to faith?

COMING TO BELIEVE

Note the place of love in each story.

First, Peter; blundering, stumbling Peter. Just three days after that embarrassing three-fold denial when the cock crowed. He's the first to go into the tomb; sees nothing but some cloths; then (according to John) went home! Peter the leader, Peter the rock on which the church would be built; the movement was over, the cause dead, the dream crushed, and Peter went home. No faith there. Later in this gospel Peter is confronted by the risen Christ. This time; a three-fold affirmation; "Peter do you love me?"

"Yes Lord I love you."

"Then feed my sheep." Two more times, "Do you love me?"

An impatient Peter responds "Yes Lord, you know I love you."

"Feed my sheep."

Notice that Peter is not promoted to shepherd. He's still one of us, one of the sheep. However, he is one who loves the Lord and is thereby given a task "Feed my sheep"!

Then there is the "Beloved Disciple;" a mysterious figure in this gospel. He is really the hero in John's church. His name is never given, only referred to as the disciple Jesus loved, or that other disciple. He must have been a follower of Jesus' and perhaps the highly revered founder of this church. In any case, when the members of this congregation heard veiled references to this guy we can be sure they knew who was being talked about, and it may be that he was the one for whom this gospel was named. According to John's account Peter and this other fellow ran to the tomb together. Upon arrival, Peter ran on in, saw linen cloths lying about but no body. The other guy went on in too, but of him it is reported "He saw, and believed."

Then there was Mary. I can't believe that she had any great concern for a cause that was lost or a movement that had gone awry. She loved him. This was deep personal loss—grief. She is so turned in on herself she isn't even aware of what's going on. So, when the others leave she just stays there, crying her heart out. To add to her loss, someone has robbed the grave. Then she sees a figure. So wrapped in personal grief, that's all she sees, a figure. "Do you know where they took him? . . . Tell me!"

COMING TO BELIEVE

Then Jesus, the shepherd who knows his own by name, says, "Mary." That does it; she snaps out of it and runs to tell the others, "I have seen the Lord."

So that's it: John's account of how three people came to faith. And here we are, Easter. How do we come to faith? We haven't seen the risen Christ, nor felt his wounds. We never peered into the empty tomb. But we are part of a faith community where the basic reality is Love. Where we do hear the call to service and are sent out in love. Where we are sometimes so overwhelmed by the experience of being loved that we hardly know what to do with it.

And there may very well be times in the ups and downs of life when we get so lost and lonely, so turned in upon ourselves that we are nearly unreachable. Then it will be time for someone to call out our name, draw us up out of ourselves, back into the love community.

At such a time we will know the words: *"I have seen the Lord."*

REMEMBERED INDEED

Well, here we are on the Easter end of Lent. The purple is gone, and we bask in the splendor of lilies and orchards and white paramounts. And now I wonder, after reciting the Decalogue each Sunday over the past five weeks, how many could tick off all Ten Commandments from memory? I won't put you to the test. But here is something most of you probably could handle: Which is the greatest commandment? "To love the Lord our God with all our heart, mind and strength. The second is like it—to love our neighbor . . ." Now, just one brief observation here, and that is, the commandment is reciprocal. It is in our knowledge of God's love for all of us that we are called to love God and neighbor. It really only works if it works both ways. It's true that God's love for us is unconditional, but if we don't respond in love, how are we to ever know his love for us? We'll leave it at that for now.

There is another commandment that, were I giving a Biblical quiz on commandments, I think few of you would pick up on. Oh, you would recall it alright. But probably wouldn't associate it with "commandments." That is Jesus' directive, "Remember Me." It is reported in the Gospels and Epistles, that on that last night before his betrayal, Jesus gathered with his followers, broke bread, shared the cup and probably other food, and told them, "Whenever you gather like this, remember me and I will be with you in the bread and the wine."

This is the commandment that I want to highlight this morning—and our own experience of remembering and forgetting. Sometimes we can be very selective in remembering and forgetting, as for example the women at the tomb. They remembered their burial duties; they remembered the spices and ointment. But they forgot what Jesus had told them—until reminded by the men in dazzling clothes. Then—click—they got it!

Let's begin by considering some of the words we might associate with "remember." There is a broad range of feelings evoked by various synonyms. The term "retain" seems fairly neutral to me, as in "file it for future reference." "Recall" is too, as in "dig it out of the file." "Re-live" and "review" are, it seems to me, stronger, but could refer to either good or bad memories. One could re-live a war experience or a wedding. "Resurrect" could also go either way, as in, on the one hand, dredging up old memories that might best be left buried. Or, on the other hand, God "remembered" Jesus in the resurrection. "Enshrine" or "treasure" are much stronger terms, evoking positive feelings having as much to do with the heart as the mind. "But Mary treasured all these words and pondered them in her heart." This, I think gets at the sense of the commandment. "When you do this, remember me." That is to say, not simply "recollect," but enshrine, treasure in the heart.

We go on then, to ponder some of those words we might associate with forgetting. "Neglect," "ignore," "disregard" come to mind. But these don't really mean "forget." Each one could be preceded by "willful" as in "willful neglect." It's more like willfully, stubbornly even, turning our backs on something and when we do that, it can come back to haunt us. "Deny" is another word in this set. Peter denied Jesus three times—then the cock crowed. There is a certain amount of deceit and guilt associated with these words. Jesus said, "Remember me." Our response can be to neglect, ignore, disregard, or deny; but, if so, we have neither remembered nor truly forgotten.

REMEMBERED INDEED

Another word is "repression." This might involve a situation where the memory of something is so horrible one blocks it out, hides it; but doesn't forget it. It's still in there somewhere, as a demon. And if we are to get free of that demon, we will probably have to bring the memory of it back to consciousness and deal with it. But, in any case, repression is not forgetting.

Still another word that comes to mind is "lose," as in you lose a pocket knife and never find it. It's gone! A memory can be wiped out, and there are some memories that should be so we can be free to go on. In any case, we are, thankfully, inclined to lose track of some things that should be discarded.

There are a couple of other words of a whole different quality that I associate with forgetting, and these are the hardest of all; "absurdity" and "oblivion." Where neglect or ignore are considerably less than forget, absurdity and oblivion seem to be a lot more. These words don't just mean "lost" they stand for utter destruction, annihilation; all reality and Be-ing totally cancelled out. If I lose a pocket knife, it may be that some kid has found it and is making use of it. But if the knife is obliterated, it ceases to exist—anywhere!

So it is that you and I with various shades and qualities of meaning, sometimes selectively, sometimes unconsciously, remember—and forget. What we remember forms us into the people we are becoming. What we appropriately forget frees us to continue the journey unburdened by sin and guilt.

But as I said of the commandment on love, the arrangement is reciprocal. We have to pay attention to how it works on both sides. We have been considering how we remember and forget. What is going on on the other side of this equation?

First what can we say about what God remembers? Let us turn to the story of the cross read here last Sunday as part of St. Luke's passion narrative. Picture the two thieves hanging on crosses, one on Jesus' right, one on his left. As the end draws near, there comes a sharp exchange as one thief derides and taunts Jesus—and the other defends him as an innocent man. The second thief prays, "Jesus, remember me when you come into your kingdom," and Jesus

REMEMBERED INDEED

responds, "Today you will be with me in paradise." Notice that there was no promise made to the man who derided, ignored, denied Jesus. Only to the one who remembered and asked to be remembered.

Then what can be said about God's forgetfulness? In 1884, the famed Danish theologian Soren Kierkegaard experienced an intense and deep religious experience his biographer calls a "metamorphosis" and most scholars refer to simply as Kierkegaard's "Easter experience." To put it very simply, the revelation that came to Kierkegaard was that from God's side, forgiveness of sins does not mean that sins are simply overlooked or ignored or disregarded, but that they are forgotten—passed into oblivion. What God forgets no longer has any reality whatever. If we truly believe in God's forgiveness of sins, we know that they are annihilated—gone. We are free of them eternally. What God forgets is gone forever and forever—and ever.

So—what is remembered or forgotten is not a simple matter of fleeting thoughts and experiences retained or lost, but of growing realities or of serious erosion; but when it is God who remembers or forgets, of eternal reality or of utter oblivion.

Well, as I say, here we are on the Easter end of Lent. How are we to understand the astounding claim that we make for the significance of this day, celebrated every Sunday? The resurrection? The crucifixion and resurrection as one total and unique cosmic event of re-creation? Christ Jesus, the first fruits and all of us as baptized participants—in Christ?

Of course we face the skeptics of the world, who variously consider it a quaint myth, a ridiculous assertion or pure foolishness. Then we hear the arguments among the theologians within the church. Do we mean a literal, bodily resurrection? Or are we pointing to a symbol of the cosmic act of God in bringing about a new creation? Such arguments have little merit. What exactly does "literal" or "bodily" mean? We can't impose the curiosity of our scientific world views on ancient writers not ready to think that way. We can't, on those terms, "explain" Moses' burning bush experience or Isaiah's vision in the temple. We can identify with them, but we can't explain them. We can however, skip the futile arguments, doubts and skepticism, and affirm what we do know. Jesus was crucified. And somehow the Spirit of Christ enflamed that early group of Christians, and in that power they went forth like a firestorm throughout the ancient world, preaching the gospel and building the church—and it is still going.

So then, what does the resurrection mean to us personally? We might think of it as having something to do with remembering—and forgetting. What we truly forget is gone, lost; we are forever free of the burden of it. What we remember is a creative force forming us into the people we are becoming, tomorrow, and next year, and forever! That's our side of the reciprocity.

From the other side, what God forgets is obliterated, annihilated, eternally gone—utterly void of further meaning. But the cry from the cross rings across the centuries, "Jesus, remember me!" And we are also reminded that the significance of what God remembers is not eroding over time, it is eternally holy and forever real.

To be remembered by God is to be remembered indeed!

WALLS AND TEMPLES

In the early '50s, in an earlier incarnation (I was a propane gas equipment technician then) I lived over there in Derby, Colorado—now called Commerce City. Those were tough times economically for a brand new family, but we had managed to buy a lot, looking forward to building a home. Metro-Denver at that time was exploding in all directions, and Derby was part of that building frenzy.

As a first stage we decided to build a garage and fit it with plumbing for temporary living quarters. The structure would be concrete block. Blocks would be affordable and I knew enough about laying up blocks that I could tackle it alone. The first step is to dig down below the frost line and pour in a good solid footer. In laying the walls, one starts with the corners, bringing the corners up several tiers before starting the walls since the corners anchor the walls. The corners must be plumb in both directions, at right angles to each other, and each block level. With the corners well started, the walls can be filled in.

The challenge then is to make sure the walls are straight, not wavy, and that the horizontal lines are level not saggy. To accomplish this there is a way one can attach a chalk line to a couple of wooden blocks. The blocks are placed around opposite corners of the structure in such a way that the blocks hold the line taunt, the taunt line holds the blocks in place, and the whole thing can be quickly repositioned on the next tier. With the line as a guide, each block can be set in place, tapped to level both ways, and the wall will come out straight, the seams horizontal.

In those days there was a certain woman in the area who owned quite a lot of land and she was out to make a killing in the apartment rental market. So she was throwing up shacks as fast as she could. At one point a friend and I stood by and watched in amazement as she and her crew laid up block walls. They set the first tier of blocks directly on the ground. They then laid up the walls using no mortar. After the walls were up, they poured concrete down the hollow cores, expecting that to hold the wall in place. Needless to say those walls soon crumbled.

I don't exactly remember when I first learned to lay a block wall. It's just one of those things one picks up along the way I suppose. I do however recall an early lesson. I must have been about eight when my father set out to build a block retainer wall. I, of course was the helper, lugging those heavy blocks, mixing the mortar in a box with a hoe. At one point (the wall was about half up), Dad stopped, backed off, wiped his brow with the back of his hand and studied the wall. So I backed off, wiped my brow and stared at the wall. He then turned to me, "What do you think" he asked, "Does the mortar keep the blocks apart, or hold them together?"

I looked back at the wall with renewed interest. He hadn't expected an answer and I didn't offer one. But I could see that the mortar did both. It separated the blocks keeping those abrasive surfaces from grinding on each other. And it seeped deep into the pores of adjoining blocks, forming a bond that was stronger than the blocks themselves.

Our Epistle for today comes from Paul's Letter to the Ephesians. Scholars are in agreement about two things concerning this letter: It wasn't written by Paul, and it wasn't addressed to the church in Ephesus. In arguing against Pauline authorship, scholars point out things like vocabulary (it doesn't sound like Paul) historic background (too late for Paul) theological issues (somewhat different from Paul's). It is conceded that it is certainly "Pauline," just not personally by Paul.

However I'd like to point to some evidence the scholars seem to be overlooking. According to other Biblical evidence Paul was a tentmaker. That is, his craft was tent making and he worked at this craft to support himself in his volunteer preaching ministry. Even today, anyone with a substantial ministry in the church supported by work in some other field is referred to as a "tentmaker," whatever the nature of that work. Well here is my (cautious) point. The author of this letter was no tentmaker; he (or maybe she) was a stone mason. This writer knew about walls and temples.

You will recall that one of the earliest scraps in the church was over the fundamental nature of the Christian community. Was it totally continuous with its Jewish roots? Or was it in some sense a new kind of community? If one took the former view as did Peter, working among the Jews in Jerusalem, it followed that anyone coming into the Christian fellowship had also to become a Jew with all its rites, rituals, dietary restrictions and circumcision of males. If one took the second position, as did Paul witnessing in the mission field, the imposition of all the baggage of Judaism on new Christians was not only pointless, it was a hindrance. The matter was finally settled in Paul's favor. Ephesians was written, at least partly against this background. Hear again the opening lines of today's lection addressed to the Gentiles:

So then, remember that at one time you Gentiles by birth – called "the uncircumcision" by those called "the circumcision"—remember that you were at that time without Christ, being aliens from the commonwealth of Israel, and strangers to the covenant of promise, having no hope and without God in the world. But now in Christ Jesus you, who once were far off have been brought near by the blood of Christ. For he is our peace; in his flesh he has made both groups into one and has broken down the dividing wall, that is, the hostility between us.

WALLS AND TEMPLES

In this "dividing wall" imagery our writer may have been thinking of the curtain in the temple in Jerusalem. Behind the curtain, the holy of holies; there rested the Ark of the Covenant—the very presence of God. Only the privileged dared enter this sacred space. This is where Isaiah, tending to his priestly duties, experienced the vision of the cherubim and burning coals, and received his call to prophecy. "Here am I, send me." Gentiles were allowed into the temple, but no Gentile would dare go beyond the curtain. Thus the "dividing wall"—that is, the curtain—not only separated Jew from Gentile, it also separated Gentile from the presence of God.

Remember that in Matthew's dramatic account, the crucifixion was a cosmic event. Darkness came over the land; at the point of death there was an earthquake, rocks split and "at that moment the curtain of the temple was torn in two, from top to bottom." In the sacrifice of Jesus the Christ, all dividing walls are essentially ripped apart; shredded!

Yet we continue to maintain them, flimsy walls without foundations and with no mortar; Walls between men and women, between races, ethnic groups and cultures. All kinds of dividing walls and every one of them diminishing our humanity. In fact, there is a point that the bishops didn't make in their recent pastoral on racism and it is the one I would have emphasized—the selfish one. Every dividing wall that I maintain diminishes my humanity. We have promised to respect the dignity of every human being, every human in their "isness"—not necessarily in their actions or their sayings, but in their being!

I was born western (in terms of world culture), northern (in terms of American culture), male, white, right handed, heterosexual, blue-eyed, and so on. Insofar as any aspect of my being constitutes a dividing wall for me against those who are different, I have diminished the fullness of my humanity. Yes, I am adult, male, white, western and all that. But that's only a slice of full humanity. Unless I am also, in some sense, child, feminine, multi-ethnic and so on, I am less than fully human.

Just one example: In my lifetime I've seen the male-female dividing line in the church breached repeatedly. Remember when girls were first allowed to serve as acolytes? Then women began serving on vestries—then in General Convention. Soon we were seeing women deacons, then women priests and bishops. In every one of these developments I found my own life in the church growing— expanding. I can't tell you how much richer my experience of my own priesthood is now that priesthood itself is more complete—more fully human—not blocked by some stupid barrier. There are still places where an all male priesthood is held uncompromisingly as the only correct way to go. Pity such people; they are maintaining a dividing wall of their own making, and humanity, ministry and priesthood are all diminished accordingly. So it is with all dividing walls.

Our stone mason author goes on. But now the metaphor changes from dividing walls that need to be torn down to a temple that is to be built up.

So then you are no longer strangers and aliens but you are citizens with the saints and also members of the household of God, built upon the foundation of the apostles and prophets, with Christ Jesus himself as the cornerstone.

Yes, we have a foundation that is deep and strong, and a cornerstone that anchors the whole structure. But what is the nature of the mortar that holds that household together? It is the love of God and the blood of Christ. And like any good mortar it cushions the space between us, keeping our course, rough surfaces from irritating one another. And it enters deep into our pores and binds us to one another for deeper purpose.

In him the whole structure is joined together and grows into a holy temple in the Lord; in whom you also are built together spiritually into a dwelling place for God!

For Mr. and Mrs. Clint Wilson; With Love, Dad

Encounter

A PASTORAL PRAYER AND BLESSING

From Platitudes and Tee Shirt Slogans,
  Shallow Piety so Unsure it must Shout;
From Suspicions or Pious Convictions that ("X")
  Is what (anything) is "All About"
                    Good Lord SAVE THEM!
From TV Preachers and 'POP' Theology;
  "Christian" Athletes, Authors and Books.
From Bumper Sticker Religion and Lack of Vision;
  Legalities and Guilt Trips with Hooks.
                    Good Lord SAVE THEM!
From Plausible Placebos and Pabulum;
  From Expositions (Simplistic) of Grace;
From Clichés and Assurances, and all "subtle nuances"
  (Intended to help in the race)
                    Good Lord SAVE THEM!
              BUT
Let Them Glimpse the Abyss with a Shudder;
  Dread the Truth of what they are seeing;
Feel a Chill in their Spine, and then turn to find
  Your great Love in the Depths of their Being
              THEN
With Faith that Embraces all Doubting,
  Love that Transcends the Absurd;
With Courage to Accept your Accepting,
  And Encounter your Fantastic WORD
                    Good Lord BLESS THEM!

SOCIAL LITURGIES
Building Community

Our life together is punctuated by incredibly important, very brief and hardly noticed Social Liturgies. In using them we consider ourselves "civil" or "civilized" or, even "polite." So, I suppose, we could call them "civil liturgies." But that sounds too official as in "government issue," and that's not what I'm trying to get at; so, I prefer "social liturgies." These are special words we use to build and maintain community. In a way the use of such words is humbling; that is, I give up some of my pride; I sacrifice a bit of my hard ego-centeredness and offer myself in the relationship—I know that I am vulnerable. Social Liturgies are costly in terms of ego. It's easy to skip or to "routinize" them.

We teach these special words to our children as soon as they begin to pick up the language. We don't hesitate to call our young teens to account when they need a little reminder. And interestingly enough, youngsters don't seem to resent such prompting to shape up their use of the liturgies. They understand.

These "social liturgies" crop up frequently in our day to day conversations and they appear on those Hallmark cards we send to a friend who has been on our mind for some reason or another and we just want to let them know. Our living together is so much richer because of these special words; I can't imagine life without them. It would be so empty, so shallow. There would be no community. We would be like beasts in the field.

So, what are these important words? Well, there are many variations, but basically, there are four: *please, thank you, I love you, and I'm sorry.* In our business of building and maintaining community, it is important that we keep some balance among the four. For example the one who is constantly apologizing; *I'm sorry; I didn't mean to do it, Pardon me,* seems to us too self-deprecating, not a very healthy person. And the individual always looking out for number one; "gimmie," "it's mine", "please," "I had it first", is too self-centered for our comfort. So balance is important—to be sure that we use all these words appropriately, and do not use any of them excessively.

Now, these liturgies having to do with interpersonal relationships, used regularly to discipline ourselves in our relationships with one another, also have their counterparts in our relationships with God. And we have liturgies for those too.

"Please" as a prayer includes petitions, requests for some favor, and *intercessions*, prayers on behalf of someone or some cause. There are many examples of liturgical "Thanks!" such as grace at meal time, The General Thanksgiving at the daily office, but most notably, The Great Thanksgiving, or *The Eucharist* the very essence of the communion service. "I love you" in formal corporate form translates into songs and hymns of praise. Consider the Psalter, the Hymnal as a couple of primary sources. Finally, "I'm sorry," which may be the most difficult of these community building phrases for many of us, becomes in this context *confession*, which shows up as a general confession in the daily office and the communion service. It is the main point of *The Reconciliation of a Penitent, (BCP)* a service of confession and absolution for people desiring it.

Let's come back to petitions and intercessions; the "please" prayers. When I was rector of Intercession Episcopal Church, we used to frequent a certain Florist Shop. I had very little personal contact with these folk week by week, but on occasion I would find myself in their plant tending to some detail or other. There was one clerk there with whom we had frequent dealings. He always referred to us as Intersection Episcopal Church. At first I found this amusing. Then I started thinking that that was a pretty good name for a church. The church on the crossroads of life; what a place to be. We could do a lot with that image.

The Book of Common Prayer is loaded with beautiful and poetic examples of intercessions; classics in the English Language. See, for example, the collects for the daily office (P 98ff): A Collect for Sundays; for Fridays, Saturdays, for the Renewal of Life, for Peace, for Grace, Guidance, and the one attributed to St. John Chrysostom! Classics indeed. These are so well known and so oft quoted that many quoters are not aware of their source. There are special collects for each Sunday, Seasons and Holy Days (p. 211– 250). For Various Occasions: (p. 251–261; traditional forms p. 159 ff). And, should this leave any gaps, there is a selection of 70 prayers for various occasions; see index pages 810–812.

Next, let us consider the prayers of thanksgiving. We have already noted the Great Thanksgiving or *Eucharist*; the central act of all Christian worship. The Book of Common Prayer includes several forms. Rite I (traditional) includes two forms (p. 333 ff). Rite II (contemporary) offers a choice of four forms (p. 361–376). There are also instructions for administering communion to shut-ins and suggestions for less formal celebrations at times other than the regularly scheduled services. Notice that the Eucharistic prayers are predominately memorials; in them we are called to remember our roots, our history, our sacred stories and heroes. We recall and give thanks for who we are mainly in terms of the mighty acts of God that brought us to where we are.

While thanksgivings will be found all through the BCP we should draw attention to some specific examples; the General Thanksgivings included in the daily offices and other special liturgies, and the collection of thanksgivings, general and for special occasions, p. 836 –841. The General Thanksgiving on page 836 is surely one of the finest examples of English prose anywhere and deserves much more frequent use than it probably receives today.

We now turn to praise; the *I Love You* prayers. It's easy to overlook how expansive this kind of material is in our liturgies. Most of the Hymnal would fit in here, plus all the anthems performed by the choir. The canticles we sing or recite in the daily offices; most of the Psalter, which, of course is used extensively all through these liturgies. I once asked one of my then very young children, why we went to church just to see what her impression was. "To sing and pray" she answered without hesitation. I was quite happy with that response.

I would have been inclined to summarize—'to offer ourselves to God' knowing that whatever we offer to God is received and blessed. A song, a prayer is an offering of a bit of ourselves, a recognition that we are not isolated, autonomous, self-sufficient beings. It is a surrender of a small piece of that big ego. Seen this way the Offertory is the very center of Christian corporate worship. I'll come back to this point. But first, a quick look at the *I'm sorry* portions of our liturgy.

Confession is looking back over where we've been and who we are becoming, and taking stock of that in plans and decisions for the future, and in so doing dumping all the trash that is in there; lighten the load so to speak, so as to be free to continue the journey unencumbered by all the stuff that would otherwise weigh us down and impede our progress. The great eighteenth century Danish theologian and existentialist, Soren Kierkegaard makes occasional reference to his "Easter experience." This seems to have been a dramatic personal insight that came to him in a flash. The sense of it, is that when GOD forgives, God effectively *forgets*, and what God forgets is gone—there is no longer any reality to it. It's not a matter of God saying, "Well that's OK, I'll over look the offense this time." In which case there might be another time when God remembers. Not so, says Kierkegaard, there is no longer anything to remember. The offense is forever, eternally gone—forgotten! The file has been purged. To be forgiven by God is to be truly forgiven, made clean.

The Book of Common Prayer provides for a general confession

and absolution in the daily office, in the various forms for Holy Communion, Compline, Ash Wednesday, and in the various pastoral offices. The season of Lent is considered a penitential season and appropriate seasonal observances are usually offered. The Pastoral Office *The Reconciliation of a Penitent* (BCP p 447) is a form for personal confession, counseling and absolution.

The old Anglican liturgies, including the 1928 BCP that I grew up with, were overall, much more penitential in tone than contemporary services. Upon entering church thirty years ago, the mood was solemn, quiet, reserved; there was very little greeting of friends. It was as though one came to church for private devotions rather than for corporate worship. Many felt incredibly uncomfortable in the passing of the peace. All this "touchy, feely" stuff just didn't seem right in the presence of THE HOLY. It was almost like every Sunday was a Good Friday. "Celebration" was not what we were about. Even the architecture fought against "community." We sat there like words on a printed page, eyes front, looking at each other's backs, rather than in a circle like a picnic in the park.

We couldn't change overnight. The 1979 BCP probably couldn't have been accepted without certain compromises with the traditionalists. So, we still have the "Rite One" liturgies, "traditional" forms of many of the collects, and other compromises. Today, if I asked my daughter why we go to church, she might still be inclined to say "to sing and pray" and that would be just fine. However she might also be inclined to add "to celebrate the resurrection" and I would like that too.

I noted earlier that the Offertory, in some sense, sums up the total meaning of worship for the Christian, (or, for anyone, I suppose). I remember many years ago, when I was newly ordained, hearing of the woman who came to her priest greatly distressed over the fact that in her prayer life she was unable to pray for anything more important than her golf score. Her priest wisely counseled her to keep it up—It's ok to pray for a better golf game, and to keep up her regular church related disciplines as well. I would have tried a more direct approach. But after pondering this incident for a long time I finally saw the wisdom in it. This woman was humbly surrendering a little piece of herself, admitting her woeful inadequacy, her utter dependency finally, on something bigger than herself. It's not much, but it's a start, something to build on. This time next year, who knows what she might be praying for?

I said at the beginning of this homily that the practice of "social liturgies" is humbling, a "sacrifice of a bit of my pride" and an offering of myself in a relationship making me aware of my vulnerability. But an offering of oneself is something that God gladly receives; there is joy in heaven and the angels sing. What is more, that offering is blessed and made a part of God's New Creation.

RADICAL DISCIPLESHIP

". . . But go, tell his disciples and Peter that he is going ahead of you to Galilee; there you will see him just as he told you." So they went out and fled from the tomb, for terror and amazement had seized them; and they said nothing to anyone, for they were afraid."

That's it! That's the end of Mark's Gospel. *". . . for terror and amazement had seized them; and they said nothing to anyone, for they were afraid."* Actually, it sounds like a reasonable account of what could have happened—but what an abrupt ending for a story!

According to Mark, Jesus' ministry of teaching and healing took place mainly over in Galilee. There were a number of women, we are told, who followed him around and tended to his needs. Then, when Jesus came up into Jerusalem for the final showdown they followed him there. When things really got hot, according to various sources, the men all abandoned him, one betrayed him, one denied him three times; another ran off naked when a soldier grabbed for him and got only his garment. But the women hung in. While he suffered on the cross they stood off at a distance and kept watch. And when Joseph of Arimathaea was given custody of the body they watched as he quickly wrapped it in a linen shroud, took it off to a newly hewn-out tomb, laid the body out and rolled a huge stone in place. It was a hurry-up job for the Sabbath was nearly upon them. But the women saw—where they laid him—that it was not a proper burial; and these women, who had waited on him—would be right back after the Sabbath to take care of things.

And so we come to today's reading; the first day of the week, sun up, loaded with the necessary spices, the women approach the tomb wondering how they will remove that massive stone. Now put yourself in their place. Forget the story as we have come to know it over the years. Just go with Mark's rendering. We approach the tomb and see the stone already rolled aside. In tears—in fear and trembling—we wonder, "Who's been messing around here? What are they up to in this sacred place?' Then, into the tomb; our eyes adjust to the darkness. The body is gone! But there is a young man in a white alb. "Are you looking for Jesus of Nazareth who was crucified? He is not here!" Then he gives us a message to take to the disciples. But we flee in terror and amazement and say nothing to anyone. And that's it! End of Mark's story. And it does seem like a credible account. It's probably the way most of us would have reacted. But if they say nothing to anyone, how did we get the story? How did Mark get it? Well, of course we do have other accounts. Other evangelists go on to report resurrection appearances; further teachings of Jesus. Luke and John give us reports of Pentecost. Matthew gives us Jesus' Great Commission, and so on. But Mark leaves it hanging.

Mark's account was written some 40 years after the crucifixion. Mark's church would have known a lot by oral tradition—concerning resurrection appearances and probably of Pentecost. So Mark doesn't need a punch line or wrap-up paragraph to finish his story. As a matter of fact, a clever closure ends the story and the hearer is home free, "And they all lived happily ever after." But Mark will have none of that—for his church or for us! His story is unfinished.

So, what is Mark's message? It's a call to radical discipleship. We are called to be radical followers of Jesus. Now the term "radical" is often, no usually, misused today, in the evening news for example. It is commonly used as a synonym for "extreme." That is **not** what it means. Radical literally means "from the roots." If a conservative is one who is basically against change, and a liberal is one who wants to modify things somewhat, a radical is out to turn the world upside down. Change from the roots up!

My kids and my grandkids are big on keeping in touch via email and its cousins. In fact, they keep such a flurry of stuff going that I can't keep up with it. But I do monitor it sometimes. Their topics include religion, faith, theology. A while ago they got on to the subject of the political spectrum and religion. (My turf, as I saw it) and I had to jump in. They were tending to misuse "radical" in the way it is commonly misused today. I explained matter-of-factly, that Jesus was a radical. That kicked off a furious round. But I stood by the point. Jesus took a radical stand with the poor, the downtrodden and persecuted, against the establishment. Jesus stood for change, from the roots, basic, revolutionary change. Just picture Jesus throwing the money changers out of temple; socializing with the tax collectors and harlots; or hear again his sermon on the mount. That's turning the world upside down. That's our call—to radical discipleship!

It doesn't take Mark long to get into this call.
From the first chapter (16-20):

As Jesus passed along the Sea of Galilee, he saw Simon and his brother Andrew casting a net into the sea—for they were fishermen. And Jesus said to them, "Follow me and I will make you fish for people." And immediately they left their nets and followed him. As he went a little further he saw James, son of Zebedee and his brother John, who were in their boats mending the nets. Immediately he called them: and they left their father Zebedee in the boat with the hired men, and followed him.

The story moves on as Jesus teaches and prepares his disciples for what it will mean to follow him. We are meant to follow the case on three levels: Jesus' instruction to his disciples; Mark's message to his church; the Gospel for us.

Mark portrays the disciples as people of little faith who never do "get it." It's a word of encouragement for us: after Easter they do get it and the church is launched. So, if we (or Mark's church) find

RADICAL DISCIPLESHIP

ourselves with little faith and not sure we got it, hang in there, for Jesus' call "Follow me" is still there.

The call is issued again—right in the middle of the Gospel and now the meaning is made clear. (8:34-36):

He called the crowd with his disciples, and said to them, "If any want to become my followers, let them deny themselves and take up their cross and follow me. For those who want to save their life will lose it, and those who lose their life for my sake and the sake of the gospel, will save it. For what will it profit them to gain the whole world and forfeit their life?

And finally, after the ordeal, the passion, the denial of Peter, the abandonment of the disciples, the faithlessness, when it seems that it's all over, Jesus' call to radical discipleship persists—from the grave in the words of the young man in a white alb: (16:7):

But go, tell his disciples and Peter that he is going ahead of you to Galilee; there you will see him, just as he told you.

We call this story, "The Gospel According to Mark." And, of course we have three others by three other evangelists, Matthew, Luke and John, and that's the way we label them too. Those are titles we traditionally use for our convenience. We don't know for sure who wrote them. But let's come back to the first line in "Mark's gospel: "The beginning of the good news of Jesus Christ, the Son of God."

That, I believe is what Mark intended as a title for his work. As we get into the body of his composition we come upon this mysterious character performing miracles and teaching with authority and prompting our amazement. But there really is no mystery. Mark has been quite straight forward about who he is right there in the title. "Jesus Christ, the Son of God." But note this too, "The *beginning* of the good news. . ." His whole book, chapters one through 16, is the beginning of the good news and there is no end. Today, we continue to live out that good news. **We** are the radical disciples struggling to hear and respond in faith. The cross of Jesus has turned the world upside down. A new beginning has been launched, a truly new creation. He has gone on before us to Galilee. And **we** will see him there.

COMING TO KNOW YOU

I'm going to ask you to give a little serious thought to this question: In your whole world of friends, acquaintances and associates who do you know best?

Knowing someone well is risky business. Being well known by someone else is even more risky; it really leaves one vulnerable. It's much safer to remain hidden, unknown, even misunderstood than to deal with the one who thinks he knows me through and through; who thinks he can read me like a book. I suppose one reason for this is that deep inside me I'm quite sure that no one can know me that well. If they could, they'd understand. But no, no one can know me that well; no one cares enough to get that close.

Knowing about someone is not the same as knowing the person. I can tell you a lot about some of my friends. But until you've met them, you couldn't say that you know them. I've actually heard people say, "I've heard so much about her it almost seems like I know her." "Almost" but not quite! In fact, I can imagine meeting a well-known person and afterward reflecting, "Now I know him; before, I did not" without having gained any new information about the individual at all. So knowing the person apparently has no connection with the amount of information at my disposal about the individual at the time.

So, a new question: What does happen in the forming of a new friendship? If "getting to know you" is not connected with "getting to know all about you," it does seem to relate to, "getting to like you," and "you are my cup of tea." But what is the nature of the change that occurs in coming to know another person as distinct from coming to know scads more about him?

Let's come at it a little differently, (same query). What is the opposite of love? Some would answer hate. But that's not good enough. Hate is an emotion, and when you stop to think about it, it's dependent on love. You can't hate someone you don't know. That would be indifference or ignorance. You can only hate where there is already some element of union. That element of union is itself love. Love demands some degree of union. If there is no connection; if there is total separation it can't be called love. If there is full union; if two or more are completely united into a single organic reality then it's one; more like assimilation or annihilation than love. (When two amoebas join, the result is a single amoeba.) The reality we call love requires an element of union and an element of separation.

So considered, the opposite of love is isolation. Love requires some connection but not total union. All kinds of things can be going on in that connection, from devotion to offence. The multitudes went out to see Jesus of Nazareth as he passed by. Many were moved to devotion, some were offended – they are opposite responses – many continued on their way unaffected having missed the encounter altogether. So it is with the multitudes today.

The connection I've called union or love is also known as relationship. Entering relationship requires risk, and the courage to move out beyond self into the space between persons. In relationship two people lower their guards, set caution aside long enough to 'test the waters' and venture beyond themselves. It's highly risky and incredibly promising. The connection isn't mechanical, it isn't organic, it is not tangible, yet it is real and experienced. It is also spiritual and it can be sacramental; but it is personal and it is called relationship. The potential for personhood in each of us is realized in the space between persons in a connection we call relationship. The courage required to come out, leave security behind, dare to enter that risky place between people in our own nakedness and vulnerability, exposed and defenseless; that courage is called faith. The attitude necessary for even daring to step out into this abyss is humility.

Now here is an interesting factor in all this: As we accumulate more and more information about someone it becomes increasingly difficult to hate the individual. More and more information about the other leads to better understanding and more tolerance of the other. In this sense "getting to know more about you," does reinforce, "getting to know you." And it moves one to forgive. Yes, understanding what makes the other guy tic definitely leads to acceptance. There is no exception. To see this, is to understand how it is that God knows, loves and forgives each of us.

Jesus visited his hometown, went into the synagogue and preached. The people thought they knew him, after all they knew all about him. "Where did this man get this wisdom? Is this not the carpenter's son? Are not his brothers and sisters with us? Where did he get all this?' And they took offense at him. This is one of those instances where the meeting results in offense rather than devotion. "And he did not do many deeds of power there, because of their unbelief." They knew all about him and confused that with knowing him. With complete confidence in their information about him, why risk getting to know him?

Contrast that with the woman who had been suffering from hemorrhages for twelve years, who came up behind him and stealthily touched the fringe of his cloak, knowing that even that would be sufficient. Jesus said, "Take heart daughter, your faith has made you well." In spite of the risk of humiliation, she dared into that scary domain and, just as she feared, was in fact discovered. Nevertheless, knowing very little about Jesus, she had taken courage, experienced her risk justified, and her faith was affirmed.

Or consider the leader of the synagogue whose only daughter was at the point of death, who approached Jesus in desperation only to learn from members of his household that it was too late; the girl had died. Jesus insisted on going on to his home anyway. He entered the house, took the girl by the hand and she got up. He ordered them to feed her. Here is a respected leader of the community whose need was so great, who swallowed his pride, who reached out in humility and connected; whose faith made all the difference.

Now, back to that original question, who do you know best? But let's reverse it now: "Who knows you best?" Many of you, after a minute's thought would no doubt, answer "God." Yes, I think many of us would say that God knows us best. Not only does God know me better than anyone, but God knows more about me than anyone else, including me. So then how do I come to know God? As with any relationship, I can get preoccupied with trying to accumulate more and more information about God without noticing that I'm not getting any closer to God. I'm only gathering files of more or less interesting knowledge about God; of more or less relevant, even more or less truthful information about the Eternal.

If I am to come to a knowledge of God, I first of all must start with an attitude of humility. I then ignore all concern for safety, security and especially pride, and dare to step into that abyss between people. There, I accept the fact of my nakedness, vulnerability and guilt and discover that I am loved anyway, and in that abyss find community.

Now, lest you hear all this as instructions on steps to be taken to come to know God, let me hasten to explain that it is nothing of the sort. It is, on the contrary, a retrospective interpretation of what has happened, offered with the confidence that it can happen again; or, you might say, offered in the faith that it will happen again. Experiencing this process personally has nothing to do with learning the steps and following the instructions. Experiencing this personally has everything to do with surrendering oneself to it.

The woman who touched the fringe of Jesus' cloak knew the truth of this personally. The leader of the synagogue whose daughter was saved also experienced this reality in person. And many of you here today know exactly what it is that I am trying to explain right now, for you have been there too.

COMING TO KNOW YOU

Spokes

It's early evening. I'm relaxing on the patio, studying one of the wheels on our Garden Way cart sitting over by the maple tree. A twenty-inch rim connected to a hub by a lot of wire spokes. One wire runs from the top center of the rim down to the hub; the hub literally hangs by that wire. An opposite one runs from the bottom center of the rim like a delicate pillar supporting the hub from below. I can look at the wheel a certain way and "see" a hub suspended by one wire and supported by another. Then again, out of that trance, I see all the wires. They all bear some of the stress, up or down or at many angles, in a balanced configuration. Any wire alone would collapse under the load, whatever its position.

As the wheel turns, each spoke moves into a different position and function, keeping the cart mobile and able to bear its load. You can get on down the field with two or three bent or broken spokes, but top efficiency requires full sharing on the part of all. You can't get anywhere with just a hub and a hoop, or even with several spokes, plus a hub and hoop.

It's a kind of community of spokes. Sometimes, you are on the top and it seems as though your responsibilities are awesome, impossible, but it's quite easy to swing that load with all the rest doing their part.

Sometimes, you are down and it looks like that load above you is unbearable, delicate as you are. But with all the others sharing from so many directions, it's not really bad at all.

Of course a community of spokes doesn't just exist for itself. It's there to contribute to the larger purpose to which the cart is dedicated. It is important to keep every spoke taut, straight and rust free. For that, they depend on outside help. No cart can do it. There are other communities, maybe not quite as efficient in sharing the load. Yet, members do have a way of fixing the kinks and polishing one another. They practice a discipline of calling on, and accepting, outside help. They're called Eucharistic Communities

SPOKES

MARK'S STORY

In the Chronicles concerning the great prophet Mohammed it is written that, on one occasion, while the prophet dictated to the scribe Abdullah, the prophet paused, collecting his thoughts, leaving one sentence half finished. The scribe, totally caught up in what the prophet was saying, instinctively finished the sentence. Mohammed accepted the scribe's contribution as Divine Revelation. The scribe however, was totally humiliated. How could a lowly scribe have presumed such a thing? Abdulla abandoned the prophet and lost his faith in Allah.

In Christianity, we have four scribes of record: Matthew, Mark, Luke and John. They boldly told the story in their own way and based on their own sources, interpreting Jesus' parables and teachings in their own accounts. Each developed themes, plots and angles according to what each felt their own congregation needed to hear even to the point of putting words into the mouth of Jesus. Each certainly ran the risk of Abdulla. But they kept their faith in their subject, in what they were doing and in themselves. We are richer for it!

Today, we celebrate the resurrection; this year in accordance with

Mark's report of things. Mark is the Gospel that has no nativity stories and reports no resurrection appearances. So what is his message to us?

The Gospel is a call to discipleship; ostensibly having to do with those Jesus called to discipleship years ago in Galilee. But, at a deeper level, it's a call to the reader, to us. And we find ourselves drawn into their story of fumbling and bumbling as they try desperately to understand and respond to their call to their discipleship. Mark never really tells us how it all comes out—whether they ever come to their faith. But if the story is really about us, how could he know? We must answer the question of how we will respond. There is no question of Mark's understanding of all of this. His opening line is, The beginning of the Gospel of Jesus Christ, the Son of God.

The theme of the Gospel is that The Kingdom of God is here and Jesus' mission is to proclaim it and to overcome the forces of evil that oppose it. It's a battle between two realms, God's and the Devil's. In the unfolding of events, Jesus appears on the scene, is baptized by John, commissioned by God and immediately goes into the wilderness to confront his adversary. He then comes back to Galilee, gets on with his teaching, healing, calling his disciples and casting out demons as a sign that he has power over the devil.

However, seeing he is so handy with demons, the authorities accuse him of being the devil's agent. Jesus dismisses that. Why would the devil raid his own house? If you are going to plunder a strong man's house, you must first bind the strong man, then you can plunder all you want. In other words he is claiming that he has bound the strong man and now plunders his house. (casts out demons). Meanwhile he teaches his disciples, who just don't get it. (But we are supposed to.) Finally the evil powers—in the form of Roman and Jewish authorities—capture him; the disciples all flee and Jesus is crucified. It appears that the cause is lost, and there Mark leaves it.

One of Mark's literary devices is irony and he uses it well. For example, when a blind man receives his sight, that's Mark's commentary on the "blindness" of the disciples. The passion narrative is full of these ironies. Simon, a gentile from the country was compelled to take up Jesus' cross and follow him. It was Simon Peter who was told, "If you would be my disciple, take up your cross and follow me." Two bandits were crucified with Jesus, Mark says, "One on his right and one on his left." It was James and John who, after arguing over which was more important to the cause, asked Jesus if, when he came into his kingdom they could be placed one on his right and one on his left.

Jesus finally dies with a "gasp." It's the same word that is used to describe the "gasp" of the demons as they were cast out. The reader is free to infer that the devil has finally won the battle and has cast out Jesus. Yet, at the same time the curtain in the temple was torn top to bottom. At this we can infer that Jesus, in his death, has plundered the Sanctuary, the house of his Jewish adversaries' "strong man." And there was darkness over the land for three hours; a reminder of the three days' darkness over Egypt as Yahweh overpowered Pharaoh in preparation for the Exodus. The sign on the cross reads "King." The darkness (as with Yahweh and Pharaoh of old) is the sign that Jesus has overcome Caesar. Finally Joseph of Arimathea, a member of the Jewish Council that condemned him, buries Jesus. At first, this looks like a gracious gesture. Yet on closer examination, it is not a proper burial. It's more of a "hurry up, wrap up the body and get it out of sight before dark." When the sun goes down it's the Sabbath.

The account is so balanced, we can believe whatever we want. Mark is not going to give us proof of anything or try to argue us into believing. It's not the way faith works. The passersby blaspheme him, "You who would destroy the temple and rebuild it in three days, come down from the cross and save yourself." Yet as Mark reports it, they are actually hoping that he will come down or that Elijah actually will come to his rescue. Then they will have good reason to have faith in him.

And that brings us to today's Gospel. The ironies continue. The disciples had all deserted him. You might expect the key ones: Peter, James and John at least, might show up and tend to things. But, no, it's three women who take their place as disciples and set out to do a proper burial.

But the tomb is empty and the young man declares, "He is not here, he is risen." But go, tell his disciples that he is going ahead of you to Galilee; there you will see him, just as he told you. Now with all those healings Jesus did, he always admonished the subject "Don't tell anyone." But they could not contain themselves and witnessed anyway. Now the women are told to get out there and spread the word, but they could not, "For fear and anguish had seized them, and they said nothing to anyone, for they were afraid."

And there Mark leaves it. No convincing "proof." No admonitions "to believe." Nothing. And we are left with the question, "What did the women finally do?" No, that's not quite right. We are left with the question, "What are WE going to do?"

Actually, for Mark this is no mere question. It's a challenge. There is no question here of where Mark stands on the meaning of this story. He was quite up front right from the beginning. Remember, I quoted Mark's opening line of this story, The Beginning of the Gospel of Jesus Christ, the Son of God. Mark's story isn't the whole Gospel, it's only the beginning.

We are its continuation. We bear its challenge.

SEEK THE LIVING

"Why do you look for the living among the dead?" That's the rhetorical question the angels put before the women at the empty tomb. I think the reason the words gripped me is because, in an ironic way, they describe us here on our wilderness trek. If the women had come here to the Highland Cemetery seeking the living among the dead, they would have discovered us and lots of life here among the dead. That however doesn't answer the question; not for the women, nor for us who, under the circumstances, seem to be faced with the same question.

Why do we look for the living among the dead? I'm not thinking of Highland Cemetery, of course. I'm thinking of all those other dead ends where we might be inclined to seek life. If we seek life in the greater accumulation of wealth, of the stuff of this world, then we are looking for the living among the dead. If our preoccupation is with fame or power or good looks or popularity or even good health then we are seeking the living among the dead. The result, as with the women, is disappointment, frustration, not life. God knows we have need of some of the things of the world and God will provide, we don't have to frantically chase after them.

Paul says, "Seek the things that are above, not the things that are on the earth." That doesn't mean that the things of the earth are bad, nor that we don't have needs, it means that we need not be totally focused or preoccupied with them; in other words, seeking the living among the dead. Paul's explanation is quite interesting, "for you have died." Recall the words of thanksgiving over the water at baptism. "In it (water) we are buried with Christ in his death." "And now (back to Paul) our life is hidden with Christ in God." In other words, real life is in Christ, the Kingdom. Paul says "above." "Set your minds on the things above." In his second letter to Corinth, he puts it this way:

"But we have this treasure in earthen vessels, to show that the transcendent power belongs to God and not to us. We are afflicted in every way, but not crushed; perplexed, but not driven to despair; persecuted, but not forsaken; struck down, but not destroyed; always carrying in the body the death of Jesus, so that the life of Jesus may also be manifested in our bodies. For, while we live we are always being given up to death for Jesus' sake, so that the life of Jesus may be manifested in our mortal flesh."

Jesus also says something like this, "Those who would save their life will lose it; those who lose their life for my sake will find it."

But let's come back to the question, "Why do you look for the living among the dead?" Maybe it was because the women didn't have any hope. They had witnessed the crucifixion. They had seen the mangled body laid in the tomb and the great stone rolled into place. Why should there be hope? If we have no hope in the things that are above, we will seek life in the things that are here. We won't find it but we'll probably go on seeking anyway. Eric Hoffer says that we can never get enough of the substitute to fill the void left by the absence of the real. Chasing after substitutes to fill an empty life is looking for the living among the dead. John says it has to do with what we love; what we bind ourselves to.

Do not love the world or anything that belongs to the world. If you love the world you do not love the father. Everything that belongs to the world—what the sinful self desires, what people see and want, and everything in this world that people are so proud of—none of it comes from the father: it all comes from the world.

So, maybe the women were looking for the living among the dead because their love was misdirected. They loved the man, Jesus, the teacher. In their grief, their personal loss, they were so turned in on themselves they couldn't refocus their love. Again, Paul: "Seek the things that are above, where Christ is." They couldn't do that, at least not yet. So, maybe it was a shortage of hope, or of faith, or misdirected love, or a combination of all three.

Luke however, gives another explanation. Not just for why they were looking for the living among the dead, but for why faith, hope and love initially failed them. Luke's explanation? They forgot! They probably hadn't ever really understood what to expect. That's why the angels were there—to remind them. Then, they got it! Luke says, "Then they remembered his words and returning from the tomb," they spread the word, HE IS RISEN.

Surely that is the key. Jesus said, "Remember me." "

When you break the bread, remember me; when you share the cup,
    remember me."
If we really do want to keep faith, hope and love strong,
    remember him.
If we really do want to set our minds on things that are above,
    remember Jesus.
If we really do want to turn away from what the sinful self desires,
what people see and want and are so proud of,
    remember Christ.
If we can remember to do that, we will not be caught
    looking for the living among the dead.

Act of God

After pouring myself a cup of coffee, I went to the door and stepped out on the porch. What a glorious summer day; crisp, clear, bright blue sky, a sparkling, beautiful time to be alive. I remembered the last several days; unbearable heat, humidity so thick you could look right up into the noonday sun and see a faint disc barely visible. Well, that's the way it is in the Garden State; in early August anyway. But today, crisp and gorgeous. I had just filled the barn with a new crop of hay for the horses, so all was well; we would enter the autumn well stocked for winter.

I strolled to the back, toward the barn, which now doubled as a garage. In another age this had been a dairy barn with stanchions for 25 – 30 milk cows. The horses' loafing area was below where the cows use to be; above was for cars and hay storage. (I had left my car outside the evening before.) I reached the first garage door, with coffee still in hand, grabbed the bottom with one hand and swung it overhead on its track. I was startled to see that it was about as bright inside the barn as it was outside. There was a huge hole in the peak of the roof.

It looked like it had been struck by a plane or a helicopter. What else could have smashed things up like that? I went outside and looked around for some clue. No sign of anything except that some splintered boards from the barn were strewn out to the east 70 feet or so. When I began to contemplate repairs, it occurred to me that I did have homeowner's insurance. Maybe that would pay something. But what was I to tell them? Then it struck me that I should have a police report. I had no idea what such a police report might say—but the insurance company would probably want something. So I called the Clinton Township Police.

In a few minutes a police officer appeared, notepad in hand. I explained as well as I could and showed him the evidence. He took notes and asked his own questions. I was dressed in my country duds, but it didn't take him long to establish that I was a member of the clergy. I also told him that no one had been home the previous evening. I had been over in Allentown, some 70 miles or so to the west, attending a spiritual renewal meeting with fellow church members, got home late and went straight to bed. Having completed the basic paper work, he decided to examine the wreckage a little more closely. He climbed up into the hay mow on top of the bales to check out the damaged roof. He was soon back down with a report.

"Did you know," he asked, "that a very severe thunder storm blew through these parts yesterday evening?"

"No," I hadn't known that! He went on to explain, the lightening had blasted through the roof to get to the metal garage door track, and then had blasted out through the peak of the roof spreading debris across the pasture to the east.

So I asked "Well, if lightening caused all that damage, why didn't it start a fire?" (I was thinking of all that hay in storage.)

"I don't know" he replied, "But I can tell you this, those exposed nails up there in the roof were turned blue."

We were both standing in the gravel driveway looking down as he finished writing up his report. "I guess," he said, a mischievous little glint in his eye, "We'll have to call it 'an act of God.'"

"Well," I responded, stirring the gravel with the toe of my boot, "It seems a shame to blame it on God just because we can't think of anyone else."

"He has broad shoulders."

ACT OF GOD

I let it go at that.

But notice where that leaves me: I have many good Christian witnesses who can testify to the fact that on a certain summer evening in August, I was over in Allentown at a church gathering, witnessing, singing praises to God and hollering alleluias, while at that exact same time, according to official files of the Clinton Township Police, the Lord was some 70 miles to the east, blasting holes through my barn roof.

ACT OF GOD

THE CHURCH'S BIRTHDAY

Our Lectionary today gives us two accounts of the event we call Pentecost and they are quite different. I suppose we could respond by showing a preference for one over the other because we feel that one more accurately reflects what actually happened, or because we like Luke's approach to things or John's spin on history or some other reason. Let us accept both stories, not as history, but as part of the legend. Whatever happened, sometime after the crucifixion, a handful of putdown, scared and discouraged followers of Jesus suddenly exploded as church; full of fire, conviction, zeal, Spirit; and they went forth to turn the world upside down.

In John's account, the resurrected Jesus met with the disciples in a closed room. He breathed on them: breath, wind, Spirit and said, "Receive the Holy Spirit."

Luke's report is much longer and more dramatic. According to Luke, 40 days after the resurrection, after numerous resurrection appearances and after promising the disciples they would soon receive power from on high, Jesus ascended to the Father. Then follow 10 days of waiting. Finally, while they were all gathered in one place, "There came a sound like the rush of a mighty wind."

Well, you heard it. Two quite different accounts; yet neither is really strange on our ears. We share the experience. Whatever kind of poetic or metaphoric language we use to communicate it, we have seen and experienced the presence of the Spirit with us; we have heard our brothers and sisters attempt to communicate that experience, and we can hear in our own tongues because we share the experience.

But I must digress for a minute. A little over a month ago I announced that today would be my final Sunday with you. And, of course this Sunday was to have been our first full Sunday celebration in the new church. Well, as you know, the inevitable delays continue to haunt us. It now seems reasonably certain that our first service in the new facility will be June 6th at 10:30. Alan and others have urged me to be part of that transition and, how can I turn such an invitation down? The Joshua Committee has made elaborate plans for the liturgical move from here to Steel Street. For most of you, simply show up at Steel Street for a 10:30 service. For those of you involved in the procession you have or will have instructions for gathering here first. You will be hearing more from the Joshua Committee. The reason for me bringing this up in the middle of a sermon is to let you know that, while I expect to be back with you on June sixth, today is very likely my last opportunity to be your preacher. The order of service for June six includes a sermon, but there is so much other stuff that the sermon can't be much more than a greeting.

My dilemma for these past few weeks has been what can one do in one's final sermon? Well, after 12 years of preaching in one parish, probably not much. So, the question becomes, If nothing new, what is of central importance and worth underlining one more time?

Let's come back to the two accounts of Pentecost. I'll take one line from each account, elaborate a little on each and then attempt to pull them together. First from John: After he said this, he showed them his hands and his side. Then from Luke: In our own language we heard them speaking about God's deeds of power. The free association button this one hits for me is right out of our Baptismal vows. Respect the dignity of every human being. Now that's something I've certainly talked about on numerous occasions, but it is also

THE CHURCH'S BIRTHDAY

189

something of central importance worth underlining one more time

But more from Luke: They were all together in one place. Who? Listen to the list: Parthians, Medes, Elamites, and residents of Mesopotamia, Judea and Cappadocia, Pontius and Asia, Phrygia and Pamphylia, Egypt and the parts of Libya belonging to Cyrene, and visitors from Rome, both Jews and proselytes, Cretans and Arabs. What a gathering of people – from every tribe and nation – and again, hear their response, In our own languages we hear them speaking of God's deeds of power.

Now I can't tell you how all those countries just happened to be represented in Jerusalem just then, or exactly what the people heard, but I think I do understand what Luke is reporting here. Luke is telling us that the gift of the Holy Spirit is everybody's business. It's the business of the 20-year-old challenged person; it's the business of the ghetto child walking the streets in fear, and of prisoners whatever the crime. It's the business of the industrial tycoon who has no time for church or charity, and of the movie star mired in money and drugs. Furthermore, all can hear in their own languages if the staging is right. Now I don't always get to set the stage, but from today's lection I do know this;

a) the gift of the Holy Spirit is for all sorts and conditions of people – for all God's children, and,

b) everyone is capable of receiving that gift given the right circumstances. I can't deliver on that for everyone, but there is one part that I can do, indeed that I've vowed to do – my part – as I move on down the road, and that is respect the dignity of every human being.

We now come back to John. This is Jesus' final resurrection appearance to the disciples. It's John's story of Pentecost. But notice John's added point: After he said this, he showed them his hands and his side. John's point here seems to be to assure us that his appearance is not some ghostly apparition. This is the real, historic, physical Jesus, who was crucified, who has now been raised and prepares to go to the Father. The story illustrates a point in Christian theology often misunderstood and misrepresented. Our understanding of

THE CHURCH'S BIRTHDAY

eternal life is that it is a gift of new life in the resurrection of Jesus, not the survival of the soul as if the soul had some kind of reality apart from the body. We believe in a unity of body and spirit – the total person – and it is the total person who receives the gift of eternal life through Christ.

So, in the appearance of Jesus to the disciples, I direct your attention to exactly what has been raised from the dead. The body and the spirit or character. This is the same Jesus we knew before the crucifixion. But get this too; the scars and wounds – these too are part of what is saved – this too is part of what enters into eternal life. This too is part of what made Jesus of Nazareth the Saving Christ – this too has eternal reality!

So too, of us, our wounds and scars; our victories and successes, our deep loves and interpersonal connections, everything that contributes to who we are enters into eternal life as part of who we are; except guilt! Guilt is washed away and we are free – but whole and unique!

I remember the story of a little crippled girl; crippled from birth. One day she asked her mother, Mommy, when I get to heaven, will I be crippled there too? Mom replied, Oh no honey, in heaven you'll be able to walk just like all the other little children. The child began to weep while mom tried to comfort her. It turned out that the little girl didn't want to be like all the other children. Being crippled was a big part of her identity. So the wise mom changed her approach. If being crippled was that important to her sense of self, she needn't worry, it wouldn't be missing.

I didn't bring this up in order to brace you for a life in eternity in which you will have to put up with all the weird idiosyncrasies of your friends which so annoyed you here on earth. No, my concern is with today, the here and now: the business of respecting the dignity of every human being in this life. Not only are we called to respect those who are different from us in terms of station in life; race, religion, ethnicity; Parthians, Medes, Elamites and so on, but to respect them with their annoying habits, ugly scars, damaged minds or bodies. That's the way God loves them – just as they are – just as we are; and that's just who we all actually are.

THE CHURCH'S BIRTHDAY

Praise God for Pentecost, the Gift of his Spirit, the great equalizer, and for filling us with such love we can enjoy one another anyway.

ZACHARY

Zachary is a two-year-old great grandson who lives in the Delaware Water Gap country of eastern Pennsylvania on a recently acquired small farm. It's a land of bubbling streams, abundant wildlife and hardwood forests—a great place for a lad to be growing up.

Zach is part of a rather large tribe of aunts and uncles, and cousins of every stripe, living all over the country. In recent years, we have been able to remain in fairly intimate contact with one another through our email networks. It's a great way of maintaining family community and providing mutual support.

Over the summer Zach has created a minor stir over these networks. It seems he has taken to talking to trees—and to shrubs—and to worms he finds in the garden, to butterflies—well, to just about everything around him. His mom, being a relatively new mom, wasn't quite sure what she should do about all of this. And so, of course, advice and support started flooding in from all over the email networks. Many could recount similar experiences, but mostly the advice was a reassuring, "Don't worry, he'll outgrow it!"

A week or so ago, Zach and his mom were taking their ease in a hammock under a big maple tree in the back. They lay there, looking up into the canopy while Jessica, in her gentle way, guided Zach's attention. "See how big the branches are." "Look at the shape of the leaves." Zach looked with rapt attention, then observed, "Tree cry."

Well, when a two year old speaks, you can never be sure you got it just right! So Jess sought to confirm. "Zach, are you saying that the tree is crying?"

Zach nodded "Yes" then repeated, "Tree cry."

So Jessica went on. "Zach, why do you say that the tree is crying?"

Zach pointed to a spot up on the tree trunk. Jess looked and saw for the first time—no, saw in a new way—a huge rusty spike driven recklessly into the heart of that tree to support one end of the hammock upon which they lay. It was, all of a sudden, such an offense to the tree, she had to get out of the hammock.

But then, a new insight about how a two year old – at least this two year old – relates to his environment. He doesn't have to use it, manipulate it, harm or destroy it. He is not inclined to possess it or control it or profit from it. He simply offers himself in some kind of relationship—of awe, respect, sensitivity—unconsciously, selflessly, subjectively, and in such a free, innocent way, both sides are holy; the tree, the worm, or whatever it is—and Zach. (We also call it "Love.") But then, those reassuring voices: "Don't worry, he'll outgrow it." But now Jessica is worried. What can she do to help assure that, as Zach matures, he doesn't outgrow it?

About the best explanation of how human relationships work that I know of comes from the great German, Jewish theologian Martin Buber. Buber was also a philosopher, mystic and (I would say) poet. He died, I believe, in 1937. His best known work, a very short, compact and poetic book first published in about 1920, is I and Thou.

Buber says that we humans "speak" two primary words. They are hyphenated words: "I-Thou," and "I-It." What he is talking about is the two basic positions we can take with regard to the world around us—other people, plants, animals, rocks, streams and so on.

In the "I-Thou" stance, I regard the other as subject and offer myself in relationship. Thus, I leave this shell of "me-ism," the big self- centered "I" behind and meet the other somewhere in the space between us. In this union I become "person-subject" and so does the Other.

In the "I-It" stance, I regard the other as object-thing, and the question then is, "How can I use this thing or situation to my advantage?" I don't dare risk coming out of my shell (for that does leave one vulnerable). I can't risk relationship. Thus, I too am mere object; a thing among things.

Now, most of us can probably see ourselves truly meeting another human being in such an intimate way that we lose ourselves in the relationship and discover, for a moment at least, our personhood. We become human in the relationship. But Buber is talking about the wonder of relating to all of creation in this awesome, risky way, and through this, finally, finding ourselves as persons, united with the great transcendent THOU.

Now, with all this as background, let us see what we can make of this strange, strange gospel: a mountain top, a couple of ghosts, weird lighting, disciples half asleep. The scholars aren't sure what to do with it. Some speculate that it was originally an account of a resurrection appearance that got misplaced in the story. Some see it as a part of the ongoing process of Jesus teaching his disciples. Then there seems to be the message of Luke to his readers, "If you still haven't figured out who this fellow is, I don't know how I can make it any clearer!" Thus the voice from the cloud, "This is my son, my chosen." And the appearance of Moses, associated with the law, and Elijah, representative of the prophets. (Jesus is the fulfillment of the law and the prophecies.)

Well, let's shift things a bit and ask what we would have done in their situation. Imagine us on some hilltop just outside of town, and we witness this whole spectacle. What would we do? After the fear and shock had died down and after the dazzle had subsided, our attitude would probably be, "Let's seize the moment—quick, mark the spot, the exact spot. We can place a monument there, the very spot where Moses stood. Then, when the tourists come, we can point to it and say, 'Look, the very spot, and if you shade your eyes just so,

ZACHARY

195

you should be able to see a faint halo over it. That's the afterglow of all that glory we witnessed!'"

So, it probably wouldn't make much of a difference in us. It didn't to the disciples. They still didn't "get it." Peter went on to deny Jesus, the others still looked forward to the coming of a new kingdom of Israel on earth. Us, or the disciples; the compulsion is to take hold of the situation, use it, win with it, impose ourselves on it like a spike driven into a tree.

We are not, most of us, innocent two year olds. We are Adam and Eve, now out of the garden, knowing good and evil, fully self-conscious and ashamed of our nakedness. Yet our self-awareness is also a blessing. Who wants to go back to some primitive, dim, apelike existence in the garden? We don't go back; we go forward.

The disciples saw the vision, and it didn't change them much. But they did go on, through fear, through Peter's denial, through Christ's death and the empty tomb. And they came out on the other side preaching the gospel and building the church. And that's our journey too—through sin and guilt; through the death and resurrection of Christ—and now, here on this side, in all our imperfection— witnessing, preaching, building!

Praise God for the privilege of witnessing in our time, and Praise God for the holy reminder of his grace in the witness of an innocent child.

ZACHARY

196

Praise God

Have you ever heard an agnostic or, for that matter an atheist, shout out on some special occasion, "Thank God!" or "Hallelujah!" or even claim to have been blessed or gifted? I have! It doesn't seem to make sense, but there it is. All people have a need to say "Thank you," "I love you," "I'm sorry," "Please," at times. It's what keeps us alive; but to say it to whom? To friend, neighbor, family?

Yes, all that; however the need is even greater. Sometimes our feelings are so big we want to go out and shout the words to the mountain, or the sky, to all eternity. The difference for people of faith is the confidence the words are heard. So, stupid as it may seem to others, we gather in community every Sunday and shout out the words together, liturgically, confident that we are not shouting to an empty abyss but to the One who hears, cares and loves. That's one need. There are others: the need to offer ourselves to something of eternal significance, to find meaning in life, the need for a loving community. Those are our needs.

There is another side to the question; the needs of the church. Americans, we are told, are especially generous in volunteerism and in contributing to worthy causes. The root of this is religion. In an increasingly secular culture, these roots are withering. The church needs us all—not just our financial offerings and our volunteer ministries, but all of us there on Sunday taking part in the shouting, the praising, the singing, in the hearing of the Word and participating in the sacrament. I can't tell you how important it is for me, to see the church full, the congregation vibrant, alive and responsive. It draws a lot more out of me, and, I think, enriches the experience for all.

Oh, we can praise God on the mountain or the lake, but that's not the point. A "solitary Christian" is a contradiction in terms. Community is essential to being Christian. We are collectively the Body of Christ. It seemed that Pentecost should be a good time for this reminder. A hand or a foot cut off from the Body is of no use. It doesn't have a prayer!

HERKIMER AND THE ARABIAN HORSE

When my oldest daughter was 12, (We were living near Boise at the time), she bought her first horse. It was a young, spirited mare, part thoroughbred, part mustang, foaled on the Fort Hall Reservation in Idaho. She had saved her nickels and quarters literally for years to buy that mare. She went on from there to make horses and writing about horses a career.

She used to ride that horse bareback (we couldn't afford a saddle) up and down the road and through the fields around our place outside Boise. A mile or so up the road there was a little donkey pastured. Charlene frequently stopped to watch the little fellow, or talk to him. One day the owners called to her to ask if she would like to have a donkey. Herkimer was his name. They explained that Herkimer had belonged to their children who had since grown up and gone their ways. They would appreciate knowing that Herkimer had a good home and was around children.

Charlene hurried home for a brief family conference. (You know how those conferences go: "Can I, huh, please, can I?" although it more frequently involves puppies or kittens). She was soon on her way back with her sister riding double, to pick up the donkey. The younger girl got on him and headed him down the road. Charlene and the mare remained behind to herd them along. The whole business was very annoying to the mare. She could have made the trip twice over while Herkimer was making up his mind to cross the road. So she danced and pranced, and when she got a chance reached out and nipped him on the rump; which did hurry him along a little. They finally got home and Herkimer went into the pasture behind the house.

So it was that a little donkey came into our lives. We not only came to love him, we also learned a little about donkeys. They are really not much for riding for example. You can get there just about as fast walking. And a full grown man will probably find that, astride a donkey, his feet drag on the ground. Not much dignity in that. And then there's that donkey bray, the "hee-haw." The donkey wasn't blessed with the whinny of a horse, or with any efficient instrument for making vocal sounds it seems. When he wants to make that awful noise his whole being gets involved. He strains and stretches, he wracks his body seemingly in agony, and out it comes, to be heard up to a quarter mile away. When you see it coming you sort of want to say, "Don't bother, Herkimer, it's too much trouble and we know you're there." But "hee-haw" he did, every time he saw somebody come out of the house, for he loved company and he loved to have his head scratched and his big floppy ears stroked.

Herkimer was getting up in years. Arthritis had set in and he didn't get around too well. So we didn't use him much for riding. He was just a pet. During his last summer with us he would bed down for the night in the open field; then, in the morning find that he was too stiff to get to his feet. So, he'd call out, and we would go out, roll him over, lean against him, then he could make it up and be alright for the day. We didn't mind this, and he didn't seem to either. However, with winter coming on we knew it would be too much so we finally had to put him down. Such was this family's experience with a little donkey; part of our lives, part of our loving and part of our growing.

There are as you well know, donkeys in the Holy Land. That part of the world is also home of the fantastic Arabian horse, the

HERKIMER AND THE ARABIAN HORSE

finest horseflesh in the world. The Arabian horse is known for its endurance, its indomitable spirit, its classic lines and its great disposition. They are people-loving horses and they are proud. They are the oldest pure-blooded horse there is and they have been used to up-grade almost every other breed of pleasure horse around. You'll probably recall seeing the Arabians in the movie, "Ben Hur." They are a popular breed in this country today. I have a reprint of a famous painting: a proud Arab prince in his desert attire mounted on his beautiful war horse; a picture of power, pride, life-vitality, fiery spirit. Yes, the Arabian horse is one magnificent animal.

Now I have a question: if you wanted to make a grand entry—say into Jerusalem in the time of Jesus, would you ride a donkey like Herkimer or an Arabian horse? It has always seemed curious to me that Jesus' entry into Jerusalem as presented to us, and accepted by us, is a "triumphal" entry, a grand occasion to celebrate. If we didn't know the details of the story we might conjure up a vision of Jesus decked out in desert finery, mounted on a proud, prancing Arabian stallion, with the people out spreading roses before him. But no, he rode a donkey and the people tore branches off palm trees and spread them on the way.

We've seen some grand entries; say the astronauts, or a ball team, or any hero in New York City; a motorcycle escort, air filled with ticker-tape, crowds lining the street. That's a grand entry. Or a politician on the campaign trail or that Arab prince on his prancing stallion—now that's a scene that would make for a grand entry.

But Jesus. Jesus comes into town on a lowly donkey and we call that a "triumphal entry." Not only that, but it does not in fact seem strange to us. We look at it knowingly, admiringly. As Christians we understand the message. It is Jesus' mockery of the superficial symbols of authority, position and status—of the phony pretensions of kings and princes—yes, of priests and bishops, a mockery of purple robes and gold crowns, of the silver crosier and embroidered stole, of the corner office and the red carpeted floor. He said his kingdom was not of this world. His entry into Jerusalem was altogether appropriate for such a king, and a profound mockery of all that's associated with the thrones, realms, titles and pretensions of this world.

But there is another mockery—the mockery associated with the cross. They put a purple robe on him. They plaited a "crown" of thorns and jammed it onto his head. They nailed a sign on his cross, "King of the Jews". As he died, they stood around mocking him verbally. And it's a mockery that continues today. We hear it in tasteless slurs, foul language or offensive cartoons.

So, we have two mockeries; Jesus' mockery of the powers and principalities; of the symbols of authority and position—then the authorities' and the mobs' mockery of Jesus as king. We stand before the first in admiration, with understanding, perhaps even a quiet little chuckle; also, at a deeper level, with awe and wonder—the power of it. We stand before the second in sadness and shame; perhaps even a tug of guilt—the awful powerlessness of it!

But there is another way to look at this: not as two mockeries, one initiated by Jesus, another aimed at him; but as one mockery. The two do after all, fit together very well. The king who rides a donkey doesn't wear purple, and a gold, jewel-studded crown, and he doesn't reign from an elevated throne. He is naked, wears a crown of thorns and reigns from a rough-hewn cross.

Jesus did after all initiate the mockery. He didn't have to come into town and he knew what would happen. Yes, Jesus started this mockery business and he sustained it right through to the end. It's not two mockeries. It's one continuous mockery and Jesus is in charge all the way. We're inclined to think of the mockery of the people as something they thought of. But they didn't, they were maneuvered into a predictable role. They were merely responding according to the script. Jesus set it up—riding a donkey—and they played their part. They were simply responding as expected in Jesus' grand mockery of the whole thing. The message Palm Sunday—Good Friday—Easter is a consistent, sustained mockery of the dumb values of this world— and the authorities and the mob and the magazine editors and the cartoonists—they help him do it!

Shall we stand before the cross in sadness and shame? Well yes, but also in admiration, and understanding, perhaps even a little chuckle;

and, at a deeper level, with awe and wonder; the power of it!

He reins as Christ the King even from the cross. He pulled it off; he saw it through. And the Cross! It just has to stand as the supreme put-down of all time; The Ultimate mockery of all the pride and pretensions of a sinful world!

DAILY BREAD

In 1884 a young English accountant named Edward set sail from England for the new world. He already had a job with a firm in Western Pennsylvania. He landed in New York and by way of the Erie Canal made his way to Sharon on the Pennsylvania – Ohio border. His wife Elizabeth would follow a year later.

In those days one paid for passage and quarters on the small sailing vessel and that was it. People then had to provide for themselves from their version of a "brown bag" of non-perishable food. And since the journey was expected to take about two weeks, that required a fairly large brown bag. This was not a luxury liner. Most passengers and crew members were seasick and there were quite a few burials at sea.

As the ship approached New York a big storm came up and blew them halfway back across the Atlantic. They would finally arrive in New York two weeks late. However, by then hunger was rampant as passengers tried to stretch their provisions to cover the delay. For a young man traveling alone this was a little easier to manage than for a family. So it was that Ed frequently saw two small children roaming the deck munching on crusts of dry bread. He got into the practice of inviting them into his cabin where he quietly covered their bread with fruit preserves and set them on their way. Such an act would probably not be memorable except that a few weeks later, Ed, now settled in Sharon, Pennsylvania, received a parcel from North Carolina. It was a white silk scarf with a note. ". . . wanted you to know that your kindness to our children did not go unnoticed. We are not poor people, but as we approached New York the first time we got careless with our provisions and then ran short." The writer was in the silk manufacturing business and was relocating in America. When I was a child, that scarf was still in the hands of family members.

Ed and Elizabeth were my great grand-parents. They were among the founders of St. John's Episcopal Church in Sharon. During the depression that followed the Civil War the new church found itself nearly broke. The cost of a rector and the accumulating mortgage payments were simply too much. Ed and some friends proposed a community dance as a fund raiser. Others in the church opposed the idea as inappropriate for a church. However, the supporters went ahead with their plans anyway and raised a tidy sum beyond their goal. The following Sunday at the offertory they attempted to present their special offering. The opposition was still alive and kicking, and managed to have the special offering refused. On Monday morning, the dance promoters went down to the bank in person and paid off the debt. From that point on church-sponsored dances have been common, not particularly as fund raisers but as part of the social life of the parish family.

We pray, "Give us this day our daily bread," hardly giving it a thought. We might suppose that that new North Carolina family prayed those words daily before scrounging around in their brown bag for some scraps for the kids, and that the words really meant something to them. Making it one day at a time really does count when the bag is nearly empty.

Among the hungry of the world, bread is frequently the staple of life. In the Far East that role is filled by rice. I was privileged to spend some time in the Philippines with a group of eastern bishops several years ago. Among them was one James Pong, Bishop of Hong Kong. He was familiar with hunger on a grand scale. He pointed out that in the west when people greet one another, the usual exchange is "How

DAILY BREAD

are you?" In his circles a more common greeting was, "Have you eaten?"

I remember a friend of mine one time hosting a Chinese guest. One of the things he did, trying to be a gracious host was take him out to dine at a fine restaurant where the touted cuisine was Chinese. As they completed their meal my friend, curious about how a real Chinese might experience American "Chinese" food asked "Well, How was it?"

His guest replied, "The rice was wonderful."

For the hungry of the world the prayer goes, "Give us this day our daily crust of bread or scoop of rice." What would we give for the chance to give a starving refugee a slab of bread smothered with strawberry preserves in response to this prayer?

In the underworld or on the street bread might be a euphemism for money or payoff—greasing the palm. Can you imagine members of the mob gathered together prior to their day on the street, praying "Give us today our daily bread?"

For many of us bread is a symbol of community. Our prayer could be "Give us this day our sacrament of real life in Christ." Jesus said that the manna that our forbearers received in the wilderness was not from Moses, it was from God. Our prayer could be "Give us today the continuing abundance of your manna."

Bread can also stand for God's revelation to God's people. In today's reading from John's Gospel Jesus is quoted as saying, "I am the bread of life." This is one of John's "I Am" passages which always echo the Exodus story (the voice from the burning bush). "Tell them 'I Am' sent you." It is God who speaks the Word. And in the prologue to this Gospel we read, "And the Word was made flesh," or we might say in this context, "And the Word was made bread." So the revelation of God continues to come to God's people, breaking down old prohibitions—against dancing two generations ago; against ordaining women a generation ago—against whatever nonsense stands in our way today; the revelation continues ever setting us free from bondage for new life. Our prayer could be, "Give us this day a sparkling new revelation that we might be your light in the world."

DAILY BREAD

We are not among the starving of the world begging for a crust of bread or a handful of rice. And we are not among those of the underworld scrambling for a daily share of the graft emanating from corruption, drug sales and pimps.

"Bread" has more of a symbolic than a nutritional meaning. "Breaking bread," doesn't conjure up images of satisfying hunger so much as fostering fellowship, community, blessings—even, in the sense of revelation, guidance in coping with new challenges.

So it is that when we pray, "Give us this day our daily bread." We do it without much thought and, really, with little expectation. How would we know it if the prayer were answered? We are already surrounded by God's blessings. Look at the abundance that's around us today. Our prayer should be one of thanksgiving for blessings already received. The prayer is answered before we pray it.

Management Consultant Peter Drucker, observing the small vision of some leaders and the tendency to always see problems and hurdles where there are blessings and opportunities notes that, "When it rains manna from heaven, most people reach for an umbrella, some for a big spoon." So let us keep our expectations high. And when we pray, "Give us this day our daily bread," have some extra spoons on hand for sharing; never mind the umbrellas.

DO YOU SUPPOSE?

Psalm 121 is a favorite for a lot of people and one frequently chosen for funerals. There is, however, some uncertainty over the punctuation of the first couple of verses. (The Hebrew had no punctuation.) Some old English versions, such as the King James, would have it read, "I lift mine eyes to the hills from whence cometh my help. My help cometh from the Lord." In this rendering of it, the Lord seems to be identified with the mountain. In need of help, I look to the mountain top—the "place" of the Lord. The help, of course, comes from the Lord, not the mountain. But still, the mountain is a "holy place." You and I know we can pray anywhere, but sometimes, (times of special need) we might be inclined to come into the church to offer our prayers. It's a "holy" place. This rendering of the passage seems to fit in with Jewish experience—their formation period at the foot of Mt. Sinai—with Moses going up the mountain to converse with God then bringing the Word of God down to the people.

However, modern translations of the psalm read, "I lift my eyes to the hills, from where is my help to come? My help comes from the Lord." In this rendering one might almost skip the first phrase.

DO YOU SUPPOSE?

What's its point? It could simply read, "From where is my help to come?" Yet this loses something of the poetry and setting. "I lift up my eyes to the hills." Sort of sets up a meditative mood and a soulful longing. Then the question: "Where is my help?" There is something about the hills—the glory and majesty of God who created them.

I have a friend in Appalachia, Linda, a social worker with the mountain people and a product of a long line of hillbillies. She quotes her father as saying, "God created mountains so people would have something to lean their eyes up against." We who live here at the foot of the mountains are fortunate indeed. How often, as I drive between Arvada and Thornton, I look to the west—the ever changing glory and majesty of the mountains, with the changing of the seasons or the angle of the sun—and lean my eyes against that towering strength.

The conference center in the Diocese of Bethlehem is on the top of a hill near Wilkes Barrie. It's a beautiful old mansion with well- kept gardens and a magnificent view all around. I've known many people who have experienced weekend retreats in that center—I've shared many of them—and it is common talk afterward, as people share those times, to speak of their "mountain top" experiences. Martin Luther King, Jr. said, "I've been to the mountain top," as a way of setting forth his vision of justice and equality for all Americans. And so it is for all people who have been to the mountain top to be somehow, at least for a time, transformed.

And, it shows, whether it is Moses, whose face glowed so that people couldn't look at him, or Jesus, whose raiment glistened and the apostles couldn't fathom it. Or the disciples, as Luke reports in another place, somehow changed so that others "perceived that they had been with Jesus." The phenomenon occurs in holy places. The burning bush of Moses: "Take off your shoes, this is holy ground." The temple of Isaiah, the cherubim appear. But often it is on a hill or mountain, as in today's readings. And even if the setting is somewhere else, such experiences of the presence—the manifestation of God, seem like "mountain top" experiences.

About 10 days ago, I took Lynne to Boulder to cash in on her birthday present, a ticket to go for a ride in a glider. She wouldn't

DO YOU SUPPOSE?

think of it as a manifestation of God, but, still a kind of "mountain top" experience. I watched her soaring overhead—over the Flatirons, playing tag with the clouds—until she was so high she was out of sight. And then, very quickly, back down to earth. That too is part of mountain top experiences; you have to come back down and get on with life. A couple of days later we got word of her father's stroke. Now that's getting back down to earth in a hurry. Moses did it. Jesus did it. The mission goes on and it goes on here on earth, not on some mountain top. In a way it's a parable of life: soaring one minute, mourning the next. Ups and downs—and life goes on.

Lynne and I had known each other for many years before our marriage 13 years ago. During those years I knew very little about her family; or they about me. The spring following our marriage we visited her folks in Kerrville, Texas, and I became part of the clan. With that, a whole new set of relationships began to bloom. One of the signs for me was when Ed, her father, began to count on me for an opinion or a helping hand. It's the presumption I guess; the relationship is strong when one has a right to presume on another. It's the stuff of family ties. Often Ed's approach was, "Say Chuck, do you suppose . . .?" then would follow some speculation on the nature of things—in technology, theology or whatever. Sometimes it was a request for a helping hand. One summer, a couple of years after our initial meeting, Lynne's folks decided to vacation in Colorado. It then became a summer routine for as long as they were able to manage it. One year they arrived in Arvada with a new stop light for their car. He wasn't much of a mechanic. Shortly after arrival he said, "Say Chuck, do you suppose that while we're here you could install this light?"

Ed knew a lot about gardening: about chemistry of the soil, about varieties of vegetables, about pests; so sometimes his invitation to speculation and discussion had to do with gardening. "Do you suppose they'll ever find . . .?"

It's a good feeling, you know. That someone has a right, is free to stake a claim on your time, energy, and mind. I always felt complimented. Last spring we knew that Ed was failing, so we decided we'd better go to Kerrville for a visit before it would be too late. We had a good visit. This would be the first year that Ed would be unable to get his garden in. Just didn't have the strength to handle it. However, he had already bought some tomato plants, just before the last stroke that really slowed him down. He was keeping them alive in their pots by regular watering, hoping that, someway he could get them planted. So, soon after our arrival there came the word, "Say, Chuck, do you suppose that while you're here you could set out my tomato plants?"

And now Ed is gone died Wednesday; funeral yesterday. Lynne will be home tomorrow. And I've been thinking about death. Now do you suppose that Moses' shining face and Jesus' brilliant raiment are like, well, glimpses? Or the shine in the face and the life in the eyes of someone reporting a mountain top experience is there so that we might get a foretaste? Do you suppose that God created mountains so that not only we could lean our eyes up against them, but could go to the top and have our vision vastly extended? Is death like soaring and you never have to come down? Is it like Jesus on the mountain top surrounded by the glory of God in the company of prophets and saints; and crucifixions and war and torment are finished forever and ever?

Well, for now, we do have to come down off the mountain. There are ministries to tend to in our own lifetimes. Our journeys go on, and there is plenty of grace and glory in the here and now to keep us fired up and faithful to our calling.

Anyway, I was just wondering—I'm a curious sort you know, Say, Ed, do you suppose . . .?

DO YOU SUPPOSE?

Biblical Index

A comprehensive Scriptural reference for this book
Eolithic Homiletics (EH) and a companion volume
Canterbury Mustard Seeds (MS)

Jn 20: 30-31		EH 149
Jn 20		EH 144
Jn 20: 19-23		EH 190
Jn 20: 30-1		EH 148
Acts 2:1-12		EH 190
Acts 2:42	MS 35	
Acts 13:44-52	MS 54	
Acts 8:26-39.	MS 95	
Acts 10:34-43	MS 90	
Rom 7:7	MS 45	
Rom 7:24-5	MS 49	
Rom 8: 37-39		EH 141
Rom 14	MS 99	
1 Cor 15:1-11	MS 108	
1 Cor 15:35	MS 40	
II Cor 4: 7-12		EH 188
Heb 11:8	MS v	
Eph 2:11-23		EH 160
I Jn 2:15-16		EH 188